On Blue Ice

On Blue Ice

A Not Very Brave Journey to Antarctica

Kim Griggs

RANDOM HOUSE
NEW ZEALAND

Thanks to Amanda Powell for her permission to reproduce part of 'Erebus.
A Poem.' by Bill Sewell on p.13; to Margaret Mahy for her permission to
reproduce part of 'The Riddle of the Frozen Phantom' on p.41; to the estate
of ARD Fairburn for permission to reproduce part of 'I'm Older than You,
Please Listen' on p.141; to Bill Manhire for his permission to reproduce part
of 'Some Frames' on p.65 and 'Deep Field Song' on p.119; and to Chris
Orsman for his permission to reproduce part of 'Piloting' on p.83.

National Library of New Zealand Cataloguing-in-Publication Data

Griggs, Kim.
On blue ice : a not-very brave journey to Antarctica / Kim Griggs.
ISBN 1-86941-576-0
1. Griggs, Kim.—Travel—Antarctica. 2. Antarctica—Description
and travel.
919.8904—dc 21

A RANDOM HOUSE BOOK
published by
Random House New Zealand
18 Poland Road, Glenfield, Auckland, New Zealand
www.randomhouse.co.nz

First published 2003

ISBN 1 86941 576 0

Design: Kate Greenaway
Front cover and back cover photographs: Chris Arcus
Cover design: Sharon Grace, Grace Design
Printed by Griffin Press, Australia

For Charlotte and Ruby, who will have their own cold
places one day

Contents

Acknowledgements

To get to Antarctica, even for just eight days, requires a lot of support. Antarctica New Zealand gave it to me in bucket-loads. In particular, I thank Vivienne Allan for enthusiastically embracing my proposal and Natalie Cadenhead for guiding me through a small part of New Zealand's Antarctica. The support staff at Scott Base kept me safe, warm and fed and didn't pull my leg too much. The passion of all the scientists I met made their stories easy to tell. And without K391C — Tania, Chris, Vikki and Lucrezia — the trip would not been half as memorable.

I wouldn't have managed to get to Antarctica without having a willing publisher. Annette Lee decided that Telecom's Xtra readers needed to know more about Antarctica; Jon Rochmis of Wired News stretched the ambit of his website a little further south; Harry Ricketts and the students on the Creative Nonfiction course of the International Institute of

Modern Letters at Victoria University, Wellington, listened to me stumble through an early draft; and Sue Murray, my dear friend and fellow writer, kept up constant email support from Australia.

My wonderful mother-in-law Antoinette Pleasants kept the family in food and clean clothing while I was away. My indomitable mother Betty Griggs did the same as I was struggling to finish my manuscript. My latent interest in the continent was fuelled when Mum's partner Harold Hemming lent me Sara Wheeler's excellent *Terra Incognita*. And I was a happy guest of my aunt and uncle, Brian and Jennifer Payne, whilst in Christchurch.

My husband Simon Pleasants was unflinchingly supportive both when I announced I wanted to go to Antarctica and later when I said I thought I might write this book. My winsome girls, Charlotte and Ruby, cheered me along with notes, drawings and many hugs, even if they did, on occasion, have to resort to pulling me from the computer to prepare their dinners.

This story is essentially a layperson's view of what it's like to visit a small corner of Antarctica. But for helping me in my effort to reflect accurately life in Antarctica, I am grateful to Natalie Cadenhead, Paul Woodgate, Tania McBride, Vikki Pink, Chris Arcus, David Harrowfield and Warren Dickinson. Thanks to my commissioning editor Jenny Hellen for her unflappable professionalism and to Jan Chilwell for her meticulous editing. But my support crew is just that; any errors that remain are my own.

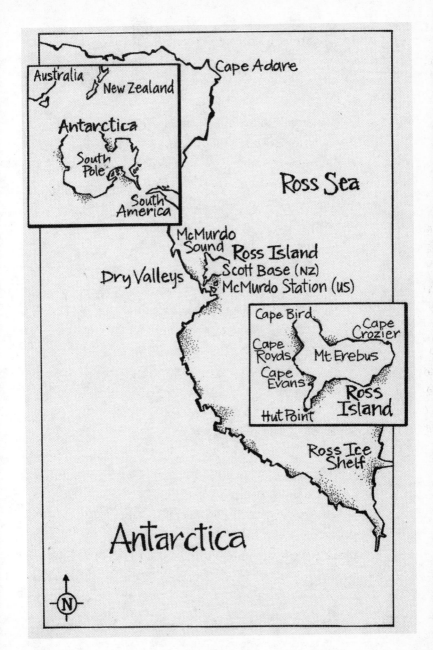

Australia
New Zealand

Antarctica

South
Pole

South
America

Cape Adare

Ross Sea

McMurdo
Sound   Ross Island
        Scott Base (NZ)
Dry Valleys McMurdo Station (US)

Cape Bird   Cape
                         Crozier
Cape
Royds   Mt Erebus
Cape
Evans
                         Ross
                         Island
Hut Point

Ross Ice
Shelf

Antarctica

N

11

1

Genesis

Always approaching:
A date, an appointment
Erebus. A poem. – Bill Sewell

TRUSSED UP IN UNFAMILIAR LAYERS OF ANTARCTIC COLD-WEATHER gear, I settled myself on the thin plastic strips that would be my seat for the next five hours or so. On one side of me was the new assistant to the chief executive of Antarctica New Zealand, on her first trip; to my right was a young American graduate physics student heading to the South Pole. Opposite us was a Kiwi from Dunedin who had taken holidays to make the trip as a field assistant and, reassuringly, an American nurse with boxes of medical supplies tucked under her seat. We became a tangle of blue and red as we jiggled our legs into the

13

squashed herringbone that would be our sitting pattern for the next five hours. I eased my arms out of my bulky blue jacket, stuffed my gloves into one of my many pockets, and examined the lunch bag that had been left for me on the seat. Already I wished I'd eaten more of my pre-dawn breakfast.

Once the engines started it was clear there was going to be little point in talking, so my US physicist neighbour and I played snap with copies of *The Lord of the Rings* — meaty reading in case of an unscheduled return. My earplugs firmly in place, I tried to look relaxed like the couple just down from me. Their heads were already resting on each other's shoulders, ready to sleep. It was only nine o'clock in the morning, but the gloomy grey interior, the heaters and the noise provided old hands with an irresistible excuse to doze. I opted for an early snack — nerves or hunger gnawing at me, I wasn't sure — and attempted to settle down to a detour through Middle Earth. As the plane taxied to its starting point, I feigned nonchalance and readied myself for the engines' thrust by grabbing the webbing above my head with one hand, as I saw others do. But, when the plane throbbed into flight, I gave up all pretence and whooped with delight.

It is enough now to murmur, 'I am just going outside and I may be some time,' to evoke Antarctica. The understated heroism of the words of Englishman Lawrence 'Titus' Oates as he stumbled out into the blizzard to die are now familiar to many. Few remember — or probably have ever heard — the final words of the New Zealand pilot who flew a planeload of sightseers into the side of the most southerly active volcano in the world. 'Go round power, please,' the captain said, as the DC-10 slammed into Mt Erebus. Later that day, all through the southern tip of New Zealand, people turned on their house lights, hoping to attract a lost plane fumbling in the dark for home. But shock waves had killed the 257 on board in an instant. In Antarctica, New Zealand holds the record for the most dead.

The crumpled koru was my first link to the southern continent. On the same day as the crash, 19 hours later, I was due to fly on another Air New Zealand DC-10 from Los Angeles to Papeete. My father, not wanting me to see the news on television, had called me early in the American morning to tell me the plane was missing. No one knew then why it hadn't come home. At Los Angeles airport, red-eyed employees let my excess baggage through for free. Later, halfway to Tahiti, I awoke with a start and demanded to know from the nearest crew member why the plane was slowing down. 'Madam, we are flying at more than 500 miles per hour,' came the acerbic reply.

More than 20 years passed before I took any notice of Antarctica again. I had partied hard in Japan, married in England and given birth twice in Australia. Eventually, the peripatetic life palled: these places didn't have feijoas, the local primary schools had concrete for playgrounds and I wanted a house with cupboards. So I prised my international family out of a beachside Sydney suburb to live amid nameless New Zealand hills. I tamed linen, chaired the local kindergarten committee, and grew close to my slow cooker. A freelance journalism business was fitted in between the school runs.

Then, in early 2000, a huge iceberg split off from Antarctica. The last time there had been one this big, the world only found out about it because an icebreaker happened by, but the path of this latest monster was just a click away on my personal computer. As I watched an animation showing the iceberg detaching itself from the ice shelf like a car manoeuvring out of a tight parking space, it suddenly dawned on me that perhaps I could visit this continent myself. It was, after all, only a couple of hours more flying time than going to Sydney. For the past 40 years or so, visitors to New Zealand's Scott Base have been mostly scientists, but recently that has broadened to include writers, artists, teachers and journalists. They can apply to spend a week or two in Antarctica, paid for in the main by Antarctica New Zealand, the government agency that supports all New Zealand's Antarctic activities. Perhaps they might be persuaded to transport me outside my suburban life and into the exotic surroundings I had always sought through journalism. In my time I had wandered into the White House press room (you only get one sightseeing trip per lifetime, I was told), sat in the courtyard of Buckingham Palace while the Queen entertained the leaders of the Group of Eight on the balcony overhead (James Galway played flute; I preferred the champagne) and met Prince Charles and Diana in a Tokyo palace. 'You're a long way from home,' she said. Then she giggled and added, 'Oh, so am I.'

Now this gigantic iceberg, levering itself away from the cliffs of the Ross Ice Shelf, seemed tantalisingly close. I had to spend a few days in Christchurch for work, so I called in to see the media contact at Antarctica New Zealand. Vivienne

Allan was perfectly groomed and, in response to my queries, absolutely neutral. She urged me to apply for a place on Antarctica New Zealand's Media Initiatives programme. To win one of the few places allocated to representatives of the New Zealand media each year I had to provide an outline of the stories I proposed to write. If they liked my outline, I would spend up to two weeks on the ice, Vivienne explained. She then politely steered me towards the tourism venture next door, the International Antarctic Centre. For two hours I wandered about, engrossed by the displays of penguins, people and assorted fascinating Antarctic trivia. A globe suspended overhead twirled on command to illustrate the polar regions' dichotomous year. Before I left the centre, I bought a map for $5; at home, I pinned it to my study door.

In cobbling together my case to be one of the journalists on the ice later that year, I touched the usual bases: I'd be writing about the historic huts, the question of tourism, the geology of the place. Thanks to the indulgence of an editor I'd done some work for, however, I had the additional lure of being able to produce a daily, online diary of my travels to Antarctica. The editor, Annette Lee, who was far less sedentary than me and training for a marathon, thought tales from a 'dumpy mother of two' would interest her online readers. Surely, I thought, a place on her heavily visited site would tempt Antarctica New Zealand. The day before the application deadline, I crossed my fingers, sealed the application envelope with one hand, and tried to pretend I didn't really care.

Barely two weeks later, I was sitting in the car casually opening the mail. We were travelling to Australia the next day for a family wedding, so I was avoiding the packing that waited in the house. An envelope marked Antarctica New Zealand was bound to contain a letter noting my application, I thought. Instead, I found that they had, with alarming alacrity, agreed in principle to my ideas. On 29 October 2001 I would fly to Antarctica to spend the next seven days on the ice. I don't know who was more perplexed in the following days: me or the extended Australian family, who looked startled when I added at the end of every conversation: 'Oh, and I'm going to Antarctica.'

Back in New Zealand, Annette and I went down to Christchurch for the annual conference that marks the end of each Antarctic summer season. I had anticipated impenetrable scientific presentations, but I returned with the importance of the Antarctic beginning to weigh on me. It wasn't just the source for our local southerlies; it was where the ozone hole was discovered; where a lake of pure 500,000-year-old water lay trapped deep under the ice; the site of valleys so dry they could be a proxy for Mars. The continent was, according to the visiting dignitary from the British Antarctic Survey, the litmus of our present, the archive of our past. 'Can I use that line?' I asked at the coffee break. 'With pleasure,' he replied. It was my initiation into the generosity of Antarctic scientists.

I was impressed to see a local journalist actually writing up a story based on the seminar. My three pages of notes were filled with illegible ciphers. I wasn't even sure, then, what a cryosphere was. 'I wish I lived in Christchurch so I could take the Antarctic course the university does here,' I said to Annette. A tall man standing nearby overheard my comment and flicked off a laconic, 'We do a course in Wellington, you know.' I would find out more.

Meanwhile, my few days in Christchurch had added other, more practical concerns. Annette and I spent one evening being enthralled by a description of the on-site field training that was obligatory for all newcomers to Antarctica. Building a shelter from snow was part of that training. For her shelter-building exercise, Vivienne, the elegant media manager for Antarctica New Zealand, had armed herself with plastic flowers and a curtain from Scott Base, New Zealand's enclave on the ice. There was no need, she had decided, for her and her companions to be completely Spartan in their ice cave, but while they were sleeping the wind blew away her interior décor. Liberating plastic flowers in the Antarctic was in itself a chastisable offence, but it was a different feminine lapse that brought that particular survival training course to an abrupt halt. Our storyteller recounted how she had informed the instructor: 'We have to return to Scott Base.' 'Why?' asked the instructor. Vivienne was at her imperious best: 'Annie's spare tampons have frozen.'

I was beginning to see Antarctica everywhere in the New Zealand winter. Three mornings a week, I catapulted out of bed, chivvied my two young daughters through their morning routine and, after dropping them at school, slipped down the commuter-clogged hill into Wellington to attend the local university's course on Antarctica. I was learning to unfreeze the continent.

Today it was meteorology. 'Technically, the interior of the

Antarctic is a desert,' the meteorologist explained. It is just too cold to rain. Sometimes there's not even enough rain to form a cloud, so droplets just hang in the sky, making what they call 'diamond dust'. At home, I followed the lecturer's instructions and stood in my kitchen holding a tray of ice cubes. My left hand held one end of the tray at an angle of about 45 degrees. My right hand was steadying the tray's bottom edge. The air close to the ice cubes was colder and denser, and so slid down faster than the air just above, giving my hand a cold tingle. I was feeling a miniature katabatic wind. Antarctica's domed ice sheet funnels such winds down to the coast at fearsome speeds. When the Australian explorer Douglas Mawson landed with the Australasian Antarctic Expedition on a sunny, calm Antarctic day in 1911, he chose a piece of the coast without sea ice. He had inadvertently found the home of the blizzard: that piece of coast was free of ice because the winds were so strong they had blown it away.

Each week on the course, a selection of lecturers took the students through a litany of Antarctic superlatives: the southern continent is the windiest, driest, coldest, highest place on earth. As I walked up the hill to the university one morning, the tow-bar scrapes on a driveway looked like the fine grooves and scratches left by ancient glaciers on the small bits of rock I had studied in class. By now I had become a geological bore. It wasn't until people could travel and look at different types of rocks that geology developed as a science. Where others admire local beauty spots, geologists turn into earthy detectives. A motoring holiday in the North Island had me exclaiming over this or that valley. It was probably carved out by a glacier, I would inform the family. 'Mum, can we listen to Shania Twain?' came the reply from the back seat.

It fascinated me that, even though ice blankets almost the entire Antarctic continent, new stories are always emerging from the tiniest fragments of rock. According to one, a New Zealand geologist was outside relieving himself when he spotted a funny lump of rock. On later examination, it was found to contain the first vertebrate fossil ever found in Antarctica: the discovery of *Lystrosaurus*, a Triassic era reptile, provided more evidence that Antarctica had once been linked to other lands. Now, nothing large lives unaided past the sea edge, but at one time Antarctica had supported such creatures. There were even trees there, adapting somehow to the absence of light during the southern winter.

It was English explorers who first recognised the importance of science in the Antarctic endeavour. As Robert Falcon Scott's ill-fated team struggled back from the South Pole early in 1912, they spent a day collecting rocks. The scientist Edward Wilson insisted on carrying the rocks, even when jettisoning them might have helped in their desperate pull for home. The 'beautifully traced leaves in layers' that Scott wrote about in his journal were, in fact, the preserved remains of the conifer *Glossopteris*. These leaves, found in India, Australia, South Africa, South America and New Zealand, were once part of the thriving forests of the great southern land, Gondwanaland.

Now the living things on Gondwanaland's remnant tend to be microscopic, but their significance assumes much larger proportions. The tiny diatom has been at the heart of a particularly heated geological dispute. Scattered along the length of the Transantarctic Mountains, the range that splits the East Antarctic ice sheet from the West, is the Sirius group of rocks. The Sirius rocks have left a light grey splatter along the top of the Antarctic mountains, a trail not unlike the dark brown splatter a cow would leave. Trapped within the rocks, high up on the mountain range, are diatom fossils. Perhaps the wind pushed the diatoms onto the rock, or perhaps the huge blanket of ice covering eastern Antarctica collapsed three million years ago, and seaways spread; as the ice reformed, it may have scraped the diatoms from the bottom of the seaways and deposited them on the mountains. It is a worrying possibility. The East Antarctic ice sheet is supposed to be the most stable in the Antarctic: if it collapsed today, the sea level around the world would rise by 60 metres.

New Zealand sculptor Virginia King had the opportunity to study the diatoms in a southern microscope. King was one of the artists taken to the ice by Antarctica New Zealand the previous season. Back home, she magnified the tiny diatoms into a strange sculptured forest and hung them from the ceiling of a local art gallery. When I approached her at the opening of her show, keen to talk to someone who had been south, she offered wine and genial small talk. But the real story were her sculptures which turned slowly as I inspected them, trying to get a grip on the delicate minutiae of Antarctic life through the chiselled macrocarpa. Ultraviolet light picked out the holes in the wood and imbued the rounded edges with a soft glow. In a corner, images of blue and white ice streamed across a television screen; ethereal music seemed to direct the sculptures through their gentle turns.

Invigorated, I started walking more or less briskly around the hills of my suburb. The medical form sent by Antarctica New Zealand was strict: anyone with a body mass index greater than 35 may be declined. My two-children, New Zealand-wine-and-cheese-body didn't seem likely to make the grade. Then there were my absurd fears: 'What if I fall down a crevasse and they can't pull me out?' I didn't even want to think about falling in the Antarctic water, where life expectancy is about a minute and a half.

As I battled into a southerly wind, I stoically reminded myself that this was small change compared with *The Worst Journey in the World*, as Antarctic explorer Aspley Cherry-Garrard called his account of his adventures. In 1911, with two other members of Scott's team, Edward 'Bill' Wilson and Henry 'Birdie' Bowers, Cherry-Garrard made an epic winter trek, managing, Cherry-Garrard recalls, to keep their manners intact. 'I'll swear there was still a grace about us when we staggered in.' The purpose of their sledge journey across Ross Island had been to gather emperor penguin eggs incubated by the birds during the dark Antarctic winter. The penguin embryos, it was thought, might provide evidence of a link between birds and reptiles. Cherry-Garrard, the only one of the three to return from the main expedition (the other two died with Scott), handed over three hard-won eggs to the Natural History Museum in London. He fumed over the ignominy of having to wait in a corridor for a receipt for the eggs from the offhand museum custodians; his *magnum opus* ends with the bitter reflection that Antarctic explorers would have their reward, 'so long as all you want is a penguin's egg'.

The polite, stoic camaraderie of the English on the ice may be admirable, but, for sheer pleasure, Framheim, Roald Amundsen's base, would have been the place. The Norwegians, who beat Scott to the South Pole in 1911, were able not just to endure the ice, but to embrace it. They built a sauna.

Winter was waning as I began my final preparations. I blinked at the bright spring sunlight as I stumbled out of the doctor's surgery, my body full of injection sites (a vital sign I am really going, I consoled myself). There was no need to wrench out an appendix or wisdom teeth, but there were undignified medical tests to be endured. The list included RPR or VDRL, acronyms for syphilis, apparently. The idea that I, a suburban mother of two, could possibly be harbouring this old-fashioned-sounding disease seemed ludicrous. But the forms warned me: no test, no travel, and so I submitted. In the Antarctic, it's not just the snow that is pristine.

My doctor progressed slowly through the pages of tests (I nudged into overweight but not into obese). Tapping the base of my spine checking for abscesses usually only found in taxi drivers or long-distance truckies, she asked me if I was excited about my trip. After all, only a few hundred people travel independently to the Ross Sea region each year, mainly by ship. Everyone else travels there, like me, under the auspices of a national programme. In fact, by now I was more anxious than excited: I was all too aware that the fruits of my Antarctic journey were likely to be lightweight ephemera compared to the fateful tomes I had been reading.

I wandered out of the doctor's and over to the local library, where I gathered up yet another armful of books. A poster in the window of the travel agent down the road confirmed that the brief season for Antarctic travel was near: it showed a white plane flying above bold blue lettering that proclaimed: *Antarctica, Just $1999*. I had a duty to at least try to bring that Antarctica closer to home for as many people as I could. But I realised that, despite having spent the past three months studying, I still knew very little about the continent. I had gone to Japan in the mid-1980s expecting to see houses made of paper; I wondered if, in Antarctica, the ink in my pens would freeze.

The closeness of my departure date was brought home by the arrival of my mother-in-law, Antoinette — flying in to look after my children. She had always been somewhat nonplussed by her Antipodean daughter-in-law. I had first shrugged off her beloved England, taking her son away to Australia, and then — just as she and her husband were preparing to emigrate in our wake — I had taken the family across the Tasman. But at least this time I could go no further south. The night before I left, I hugged the children especially tight; they didn't understand quite how foreign it would be, but I did. 'What if something happens to me?' I wailed to Simon, my husband. 'It won't,' he said kindly, enveloping me in a hug, 'but is your life insurance up to date?'

The laconic Woody, Antarctica New Zealand's movements controller, scooped me up at Christchurch Airport, home to the International Antarctic Centre. 'That Hercules starting up is heading for the ice,' he said, gesturing toward the airfield as we drove past. 'And that one there is yours,' he said, pointing to a droopy-winged Starlifter. It was, he assured me, a better flight. The Starlifter had a toilet, not just the bucket that passengers on a Hercules used. I suggested that perhaps I would be missing out on some vital part of the Antarctic journey. 'There are certain things you don't need to experience,' replied Woody firmly.

At the clothing depot, I was given the newcomer's tour. A series of maps along the hallway drew viewers ever closer to their destination: first the continent, then New Zealand's Ross Sea region, and then the area around New Zealand's Scott Base. Around the corner was the *pièce de résistance*, a scale model of Scott Base, showing the clutch of green buildings that were to be my home for the next week.

In a changing room I saw, with a start, the label 'Kim G' identifying my clothing. Shaun guided me through the clothing routine. There was a bewildering array of choice: a gaiter to protect the neck, two types of hat, several pairs of gloves, thermal underwear, socks and fleecy, windproof salopettes — a kind of dungaree worn by skiers. A huge, bulky blue coat went over it all. The air trapped between these many layers of clothing would become the buffer between my body and the cold. I was told I must wear the extreme-cold-weather gear (blue for Kiwis, red for Americans) on the plane. It might be blowing 40 knots and be minus 20 degrees Celsius when we landed. 'This is all you are going to have,' Shaun warned.

My feet were introduced to mukluks, knee-high boots first designed by the Inuit for the northern cold, and Sorels,

Canadian boots made for a lighter terrain that felt dainty by comparison. The mukluks had a quilted wool inner lining. Inside them we wore a second quilted inner lining — booties for adult feet — and socks. In the end, I hardly ever wore my Sorels, after quickly mislaying them among all the other pale brown pairs at the base's back door. I wish I had known to bring coloured laces to tie onto the backs of the boots for quick identification. It was little things like that — and slip-on shoes for inside wear — that kept the transition between the base and the cold outside world smooth.

The solitary concession to being female in the standard issue of clothing was the Freshette '4-2-P'. It was, the packet gushed, for women 'who dare to dream, who dare to be themselves'. The Freshette's pink trough and white extension tube enables women to mimic the male way of peeing. I didn't think that peeing like a man was 'daring to be myself' but this was standard issue, and the alternative had to be worse. Later, at the base, we were taught how to use the Freshette. The trick was to ensure you had a full bladder before slipping the soft pink trough into position — then the stream of waste water was propelled swiftly out of the extension tube. In no time, I became adept at using the 4-2-P and could even add a masculine swish to my hips, to get rid of drips. I made Shaun, whose smile told me he'd seen it all before, take photos of me holding my very own Freshette.

Next, Woody briefed me on the following morning's routine. Being late for the 6:30 a.m. flight would mean waiting for the next one. The final stage briefing video, entitled *Caring for the Environment in Antarctica*, set out the rules for everything — right down to how close to approach a penguin. It turns out that the flapping penguin arm movements that had so amused Scott's photographer Herbert Ponting were, in fact, the thrashings of a terrified creature. I picked up the two bags I was allowed for the week, promised to be back early, and left thinking I had managed this first step without making an idiot of myself. But, as I unpacked the clothing back at my billet at my aunt and uncle's house, I found I had lost my most expensive investment, a new digital camera.

'Umm, did I leave my camera with you guys?' I asked Shaun over the phone, trying to sound unruffled. He gently ribbed me before letting me know it was there. Before I left my aunt and uncle's house, I borrowed two brown shoelaces and tied them to the camera case so I could snuggle the case between my layers of clothing to keep the batteries warm.

That afternoon, to kill time, we visited the Canterbury Museum, where I compared my nose with the magnificent specimen on the bust of South Pole conqueror Roald Amundsen. Woody had told me that it was good luck to rub Amundsen's nose. I wasn't sure if he had been pulling my leg, but, just to be on the safe side, when the security guard wasn't looking, I gave the already shiny proboscis a quick stroke.

Antarctic flights leave early, so 5 a.m. the next morning found me struggling into my cold-weather gear and nervously checking that I had everything in the right place. I still wasn't sure what the right place *was*. Stuffed into the many external pockets were my gloves, a hat, a book to read and notebooks and pencils — black, in case I dropped them in the snow. I wasn't even sure I had the salopettes on the right way round.

Wearing all my heavy extreme-cold weather clothing, or ECWs as they were called, allowed me to fit some 'civvy' clothing and mementoes from home in one of my two bags. I had packed earrings, one photo of the family perched on a windswept Wellington rock, and my brand-new dictionary of Antarctic words. It was a struggle to lever myself and my bags into my aunt and uncle's four-wheel drive for the short trip to the airport.

I was one of the first waiting in the gloomy early morning light outside the closed door of the departure area. The sign over the door said *United States Antarctic Program Passenger Terminal*. It was at the end of the nondescript white building where I had been kitted out the day before. A few more people arrived, some in blue for New Zealand; Americans turned up in red, or the brown dungarees — called Carharts — reserved for manual workers.

Today I was leaving New Zealand . . . and, then again, I wasn't. I had my documentation — 'Departure Card to Antarctica' it said in bold letters — and my passport. In fact, any form of identification would have done for the airport formalities, but I wanted to get my passport stamped at Scott Base. The company from which I eventually managed to buy travel insurance did not believe me, but going to Antarctica is, in a way, an internal flight. The part of Antarctica to which I was going, the Ross Dependency, has been part of New Zealand since 1923. The British handed a huge slice of Antarctica to New Zealand for safe keeping — almost casually, writes historian Malcolm Templeton. But, since the Antarctica Treaty came into force more than 40 years ago, the claims of

New Zealand and those of six other countries have gone into limbo. They aren't really being enforced, but they are still retained. No country resiles from its claims, but no one else recognises them. In diplomatic terms, it's called 'constructive ambiguity'. It is the motif of pretty much everything about Antarctic life.

New Zealand's legal hold remains light, but tenacious. A baby born in the Ross Dependency — not that there has ever been one — would be eligible for New Zealand citizenship. For diplomatic consumption, New Zealand calls the region the Ross Sea region; the term Ross Dependency is delicately shelved. Within the governmental structure, it is the outward-looking Ministry of Foreign Affairs, rather than some internal agency, such as the Department of Conservation, that oversees New Zealand's southern activity. Even before there was an official New Zealand presence on the ice, a civil servant in Wellington had been appointed as the administrator of the Ross Dependency. He had, noted Sir Edmund Hillary when preparing for his exploration of the continent, 'no apparent duties and no likelihood that he would ever set foot in his territories'. The administrator represented New Zealand's Governor-General who also wears the mantle of Governor of the Ross Dependency. Now her representative on ice is the Scott Base manager each season. During my stay, the base manager and officer of the Government of the Ross Dependency was the affable Mike Mahon. His position imbued him with the powers of a justice of the peace and a coroner. Just a hundred or so New Zealanders have held this anachronistic post, but the trappings and duties of power are low key. All I ever saw Mike do that was vaguely official was stamp my passport.

Whatever the status of New Zealand's abeyant territorial claim, the reality is that the tiny New Zealand base could not possibly lord it over non-claimants, particularly its US neighbour in Antarctica, and nor would it want to. Back in 1959, when the Antarctic Treaty was signed in Washington, preserving Antarctica for peace and science forever was the prize. During the 40-odd years since, the treaty has withstood many challenges and often seemed immune to the conflicts raging without. During the Falklands war in the South Atlantic, British and Argentinian representatives met in Wellington to debate the future of Antarctic minerals. Even through the most difficult days of US-New Zealand relations, the Antarctic relationship has never wavered.

The relationship, according to Antarctica New Zealand, has been like a long marriage. The Americans were the first to establish a modern base on Ross Island; McMurdo now sprawls near the hut Captain Scott erected at Ross Island's Winter Quarters Bay. Then, as now, the explorers made a practical choice of location. In summer, this was as far south as it was possible to sail. In 1957, the New Zealand team that would support the first successful land traverse of Antarctica had been considering establishing a base on the mainland's Butter Point. The Americans suggested to the New Zealand team's leader, Sir Edmund Hillary, that he consider Ross Island. From a helicopter, Hillary looked down at the gentle slopes of the future Scott Base site, just a 10-minute ride away around the hill from McMurdo, and agreed. On the ice, any artificial divisions tend to dissolve. In the Ross Dependency, life is lived on New Zealand time, but is driven on the American right.

The doors of the passenger terminal building opened, and I said farewell to my aunt and uncle and joined the now growing, noisy queue. Many clearly knew each other, but I still had not met anyone else I would be travelling with. At the check-in, US personnel examined our bags and I was weighed. No one escaped the sniffer dogs that took an olfactory stroll around every bag. It seemed surreal that anyone might crave any more excitement than the Antarctic landscape promised, but these military men were serious. I reached the front of the queue and my departure card was exchanged for the equivalent of a boarding pass, slung dog-tag-style around my neck.

In the departure lounge, I sat near others clad in blue. We smiled and nodded at each other in the short time before the flight briefing started. An American sergeant reminded us sternly that knives, scissors, or indeed anything sharp and dangerous, were prohibited in carry-on baggage. Tighter security in the wake of the still recent terror attacks in the US that September had reached the ice. It was a familiar patter, but with a reassuring directness. If we had to evacuate the plane, the sergeant advised us, the crew would push us out.

Next came the first of what would be many safety briefings. As the video *Staying Safe on the Ice* started, an English-accented voice intoned Scott's words on reaching the Pole as images of Antarctica unravelled across the screen: 'Great God! This is an awful place.' Scott and four others had walked across the polar plateau to the South Pole, hauling all their supplies behind them, only to find that the Norwegian explorer Roald Amundsen and his four team-mates had arrived there a month before them. The hazards facing modern-day visitors exploring Antarctica, it seemed, were likely to extend only to the intricacies of strapping on seatbelts in several different types of helicopters. Learning to differentiate between the various shades of urine our bodies could produce was also a must; light fluid was okay, but pee the colour of strong tea was a sign of dehydration.

After the briefing, we broke for coffee and for the first time I met my official minder, Natalie. She had a broad smile which, in my nervousness, I found only vaguely reassuring. My other companions for the next eight days were all teachers: the New Zealanders were tall, genial Chris, our solitary male; Vikki, with her tinkling laugh; and Tania, who at first glance seemed to be quite reserved. From Italy, still looking incredibly jet-lagged, was Lucrezia. Tania, Lucrezia and I headed off for a coffee at the barely open café at the tourist centre, and stumbled through introductions. There were now only about 15 minutes before we were due to leave. Natalie came over to corral us for departure. I wondered how Lucrezia would cope with instructions out on the ice when her uncertain grasp of English left her struggling to understand that we had to return to the departure lounge.

It was time to go. Woody, the only staffer at Antarctica New Zealand who saw everyone who left for the ice, was there making sure we left nothing behind. 'Get out of here,' he said with a smile. Our dog-tag boarding cards were taken from us, and we were weighed yet again, before our busload of Kiwis and Americans crossed to the Starlifter squatting on the Christchurch tarmac. Sharing flights is another way the US and New Zealand are enmeshed in Antarctica: the New Zealand government waives airport fees in Christchurch; the US maintains the ice runway. New Zealanders travel on the Starlifters and New Zealand chips in 15 Hercules flights each season.

Rather grudgingly, the crew allowed us to pose briefly for a photo by the steps of the plane. The plane was an austere grey beast, devoid of the usual row of passenger windows. The only decoration on the fat fuselage was a neatly painted row of penguins beside the door, notches in the plane's Antarctic belt. The American crew, all hugging their brown leather jackets against a Christchurch wind, hustled us onto the plane. As we boarded, a crew member was filming us on a video camera. It was the first trip for this crew, so I put the filming down to the same touristic motivation that prompted my quick snaps. Chris thought that the careful framing of each passenger suggested more official concerns.

Loading was done in strict order: men at the back, next to the portable urinal; women to the front, beside the crew toilet. An older group of New Zealanders, who were Antarctica New Zealand's Distinguished Visitors that week, sat at the very front. It was the slightest of privileges in such a cramped place. Plastic webbing formed the long bank of seating down the side of the plane. In the middle, two more rows were pressed back to back and there was a fourth row against the opposite wall of the plane. The rows stopped short about halfway down the plane; the rest of the cavernous interior was stacked with cargo. We were allocated 50 centimetres of space each on the webbing. So that my jacket didn't encroach on my neighbour's allocation, I followed newly taught etiquette and waited until she sat down. With our shoulders squeezed together, our jackets stayed cowled around us, offering some comfort against the plastic and metal of the plane.

Jostling into place next to me was another newcomer, Michelle, while opposite me sat Marj, who was on a long-awaited return visit. On the other side of me was a graduate physics student heading for the South Pole. She was a pretty young woman in her 20s whose long, blonde, shiny hair could have served as a shampoo advertisement. Her face lit up when she started to explain the project she was working on. 'Have you heard of Amanda?' she asked. 'I don't think so,' I said, confused as to whether this was a name or yet another Antarctic acronym (which is what it was: Amanda stood for Antarctic Muon And Neutrino Detector Array). Deep within the ice cap at the South Pole, a team of scientists was chasing ghosts that come from the very edge of the universe. The scientists wanted to find subatomic particles called neutrinos, my neighbour explained, but these particles have so little mass that measuring them as they pass through Earth is an astronomical challenge. However, when the virtually invisible neutrinos stream through a mass, such as rock or ice, they create another type of particle, a muon. These muons emit traces of light and it is these traces that the scientists can detect by poking an array of telescopes *into* the pellucid ice at the South Pole. My neighbour was heading south to help calibrate the instruments for the season's work; the head of her team thoughtfully handed her something to read on the flight, a manual on lasers.

The more usual small talk of plane strangers seemed mundane after that, so I was glad when the engines started and it became impossible to chat. Earplugs firmly in place, practised travellers pulled out a book or closed their eyes to sleep. My near neighbours, the Distinguished Visitors — or DVs as everyone called them — were, to a man, reading business literature: one cradled *Jack*, GE chief executive Jack Welch's autobiography; another *Battle of the Titans*, the history of a behemoth New Zealand company and the men who controlled it; and one managed to spread before him the pages of the pre-eminent Australasian business newspaper, the *Australian Financial Review*.

For one decade of my life, I had worked as a financial journalist, delighting in the pricing details of anything from pork bellies to British pounds. Now I despaired at what seemed to be prosaic choices; even the selection of reading matter for an Antarctic flight seemed to me momentous. As the plane began to taxi, I mimicked those who grabbed the webbing above their heads, in order to not slide into their neighbours. I had been jotting notes constantly, to the amusement of those near me. Now, as the nose of the plane started to lift slowly and the wheels disengaged from the runway, the nurse opposite noted my lack of a watch. 'It's 5 to 9,' she yelled across to me. I dutifully scribbled the figures down and grabbed for the webbing again.

Trapped in the plane's grey limbo, it was hard to tell that we were moving without the usual scudding of clouds animating the windows. There were four small portholes, but I was jammed too tight to push my way through the sandwiched legs to reach one. I tried not to think of the swells of the Southern Ocean below, the roughest patch of water in the world. To pass the time, I read and munched through the first of many muesli bars I would eat in my time south.

Eventually, in the interests of research, I decided to brave the women's toilet. Testing the selection of hand lotions in the toilets had been one of the pleasures of my first ever overseas flight at age 14; using the grimy toilet on a military plane was, by comparison, an offbeat thrill. Afterwards, I couldn't face squashing back into my seat just yet and decided to stand and attempt to chat over the engine noise to the crew, who were spending the five-hour trip standing at the front of the plane. I inveigled my way into the cockpit, and was reassured to find it jammed with people; there were three engineers, three pilots and two navigators. The extras were the instructors. Flying had once been a passion of mine. At 16, I had learnt to fly solo and at 20 I had passed the test for a restricted licence for private flying. Few of the instruments in front of me were familiar, but the quiet concentration of the crew was. I was grateful when someone gestured to me to sit in a seat behind one of the pilots, who welcomed me with a radiant Californian smile. His surname, he explained, as I took notes, was Boucher: butcher in the French of his ancestors. The captain's surname was Kishi; he was an American of Japanese descent. The crew felt suitably multinational as we headed towards the world's only truly international continent.

We were flying at 37,000 feet and were already past 60

degrees south. After that latitude, magnetic guidance no longer worked, the co-pilot told me. Instead, he used a grid overlay that seemed to have us pointing north. My slim grasp on navigation failed at about that point, so I was reassured when he showed me a digital map that was also plotting our course. Everything seemed to be in duplicate on this plane: McMurdo air-traffic control fed in information, as did a satellite signal to the plane. 'If one goes down, we've got the other,' the impossibly young-looking pilot assured me.

We had passed the point of no return. Through the cockpit window I could see dark blue veins of water serrating the white façade below; the milky white was, I realised, my first glimpse of ice. More people were waiting for a turn in the cockpit, so I reluctantly made my way back into the interior of the plane and settled in to await our descent.

We strapped seatbelts around our laps, following the instructions bellowed at us over the engine noise. I wasn't sure what to expect as we descended towards earth once again. Except that it wasn't earth, per se, we were descending towards. Our 180,000 kilos of plane, people and cargo were being entrusted to a two-metre-thick veneer of sea ice covering McMurdo Sound. I kept my fingers discreetly crossed. Deprived of a view, I found the occasional changes in engine noise disconcerting, but the nose finally pulled up and we sank slowly downward. In the end, the landing in Antarctica wasn't much different from any other. A gentle bump signalled the impact of wheels on ice. It was only later that I found out that the arrival of a plane makes the runway bounce.

At last the engines were silenced and we could escape the

aural battering. It was two o'clock in the afternoon; the flight had taken just an hour longer than expected. In the gloom of the plane, I had wrangled my arms back into my jacket, pulled on my gloves and hat and picked up my bags. I tried to be as quick as those old hands further down the plane in order not to hold anyone up, but I had to ask one of my neighbours for help doing up my jacket before making the short shuffle towards the door and down the steps. 'Don't slip,' I thought, almost forgetting to look up.

I took my first Antarctic breath. It was a glorious day.

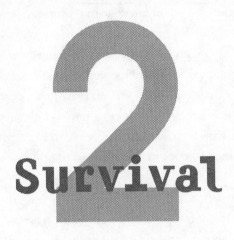Survival

Once you have seen those mountains
there is no waking up from them.
They are in your head for always.
The Riddle of the Frozen Phantom – Margaret Mahy

BELOW A TAUT BAND OF LIMPID BLUE ANTARCTIC AIR WAS THE VAST ice plain of the Ross Ice Shelf. On the left was Mt Erebus, with its wispy flourish of smoke, and on the right a line of mountains divided sky from ice. The air was minus 20 degrees Celsius and still. The utter clarity of the scene had erased from my mind the geography I had learnt from the map hanging on my study door for most of the year. Eager to call my overwhelmed mind back to order, I turned to Natalie. 'What are those over there?' I asked, gesturing towards the mountain range. 'Oh, mountains,' she said, vaguely. We weren't going to linger.

My brief ecstasy blunted, we newcomers were divided among the jumble of utes that had driven out to meet the Kiwis. The DVs, accorded a status that seemed out of place in the level plains that greeted us, were given their own van for the journey back to base. We heaved our luggage into the back of the utes before clambering into a cabin perched high above fat wheels. It was becoming obvious that Antarctica made few concessions to anyone, least of all those of us who are short.

The Americans boarded a bulky red bus lifted off its haunches by rotund black tyres. The name *Ivan the Terra Bus* was emblazoned on the side. Everything the Americans did in Antarctica seemed to be on one scale: huge. Even the airfield was big, with its clutch of container-shaped buildings. On the sea ice runway, there seemed to be as many — or probably even more — Hercules planes than the New Zealand Air Force. The US was using ski-equipped Hercules in its efforts to rebuild the South Pole station (the dome-shaped building that covered much of the current US base was being inexorably covered by snow). A new building sitting on the ice would have legs that could be jacked up and — for the first time — windows.

We drove in convoy along the flagged sea ice road and quickly through the brown sprawl of the US base, McMurdo Station. Then we were heading around the hill that enshrines the memory of Robert Scott. The expansive view from this summit gave Observation Hill its name a hundred years ago, when Scott first arrived here. On the peak stands a cross commemorating the death of the English explorer and the four others he took to the Pole. As epitaph, the surviving members of Scott's team had chosen the last line of Tennyson's poem 'Ulysses': *To strive, to seek, to find, and not to yield.* The fervour over Scott never seems to wane elsewhere, but here pragmatism rules. For 10 years the side of this hill was home to a nuclear reactor; Nukey Poo, as the locals called it. Thousands of tonnes of dirt had been scraped away from this hill, and 100 barrels of radioactive dirt was shipped back to the United States when the plant was shut in 1972.

The road swung around and along the ridge. A roadside sign, adorned with a possum, read, 'Welcome to Scott Base. Capital of the Ross Dependency. Pop 10.' Down the hill we could see the lime green buildings of Scott Base. In the absence of white picket fences and rolling hills, the buildings set up an echo of another, more verdant landscape. A former head of the Antarctic programme had wanted the base to have a more uniform appearance than the various shades of yellow it started out with. His tenure (1965–88) and name (Robert Baden Thompson) lives on in his colour scheme. The shade will forever be known as RBT green.

The utes bumped to a halt outside their hitching rail: they had to be plugged in so that fans could keep the motors from freezing when they were not in use. Inside the back door we went through the first of many gear unbundlings, trying to commit to memory where we put our stuff. The name tag on my jacket began to make sense.

Visitors to the base were accommodated in bunk rooms in 'Q' Hut, four or six to a room. It was relatively new and handily adjacent to the library and the loos, but the rooms must have been designed by men, and very tall ones at that. I would have needed a step-ladder to reach the impossibly high clothing rail in the wardrobe allocated to me and so ended up piling all my extreme-cold-weather clothes on the wardrobe floor. My small selection of make-up was dumped into a filing cabinet that served as a set of drawers. The room designers plainly hadn't anticipated visitors who indulged in frivolities such as make-up; the only mirror in the room was just the right height for a man to run a comb through his hair. I tucked my bedtime reading, an optimistic addition to my luggage, beside my bed, and shoved the rest of my clothing into drawers underneath my bunk. My family smiled out from a photo mounted high up, virtually invisible, on top of the filing cabinet. At least I had a bottom bunk away from the door.

The lack of feminine comforts wasn't really surprising; the base had been the preserve of men for so long. It wasn't until the late 1960s that the first woman came to Scott Base to spend a summer season and it was the late 1970s before a woman stayed for the winter. But those on base did try to ease our newcomers' feelings of unfamiliarity. On my pillow, bringing me into the fold, was a little blue booklet. It outlined the rules of life on the base, but, most warming of all, it had my name scrawled on the cover: *Antarctica New Zealand welcomes Kim to Scott Base 2001/2002.*

Sharing my room was Marj, who was heading to Cape Hallett, and Michelle who had sat beside me on the plane. On the first night we also shared with a scientist who was heading to another part of Antarctica the next day. A whiteboard on the room's door allocated each of us one of the four beds. Poor Marj had to sleep on a bed that positioned her head right next to the door. For a light sleeper like her, this was torture. As was the constant sunshine that leaked into the room, even with the shutters pulled over the two small windows. I wasn't a good room-mate, with my catarrh and nasal noise, and the next morning she growled at me the moment I was awake: 'Did you know you snored?'

The various green buildings were all linked with corridors. Once, these linkways had been unheated and old-timers write of sprinting through icy connections between the huts. Now it was a pleasant stroll from one area to the next. I walked out of my room and across the hallway to the laundry, showers and toilets. To the right was the laboratory, where I could set myself up to work. Just along from our room and up some stairs was the library.

In the heart of the base were the mess and the bar. Scott Base has never been run by the military, but many New Zealand defence personnel have had postings here. That flavour comes through in the terminology, the briefings and in the bar. That, and the shop, are run by the Armed Forces Canteen Council. Through one of the elongated windows in the mess I spied the New Zealand flag. When the New Zealand flag was first raised here in 1957, it was hoisted up a flagstaff that had been used by Scott at Hut Point. This honour fell to the youngest member of that New Zealand team, 20-year-old A.B. Ramon Tito. In my teenage years, I had been ignorant of the Antarctic history just over the road; the Titos were our neighbours for years as I grew up in Rotorua.

Next to the flag-pole are the much-photographed yellow and black road signs showing the distance in kilometres to places such as London, Moscow and Tokyo. The closest destination was the South Pole, a mere 1353 kilometres away. My home town, Wellington, was 4080 kilometres away. At the junction between the track to the base and the road to the hill, another sign directed drivers to 'McMurdo Station (United States)', 'Scott Base (New Zealand)' and the landing strip that would be used later in summer, 'Williams Field (United States)'. Out the front of the base another plank proclaimed: *Scott Base New Zealand Lat 77°51′ South*. Each of our little team had photos taken of themselves next to these signs — anchors in a white world. They provided some bearings in a landscape that transcended any of the usual trappings of human geography.

The base, I decided that first evening, was a cross between a well-appointed ski lodge, a boarding school, and the American sitcom *M*A*S*H*. My team-mate Chris was reminded of the English holiday camps parodied on television. Booming announcements over the Tannoy system — 'Bags from today's flight will be at the back door in 10 minutes' — only reinforced his first impression. Our team, who had been sprinkled throughout the bunkrooms, met in the hallway to reclaim our green holdalls. Unpacking finished, Chris, Tania, Lucrezia, Vikki and I reassembled in the mess for dinner.

A queue always formed at the start of each mealtime. It wasn't that anyone would miss out — you could always help yourself to a sandwich — but working in the cold seemed to sharpen the edge of your hunger. The chef, Jeff, had a mop of blond curly hair with vestiges of green dye in it. He turned out to be one of those guys who can party voraciously but still manage, with the aid of the other chef, Clare, to turn out superb meals every three or four hours during the day. The mornings got underway to the smell of freshly cooked bread. Morning tea was a variety of scones or muffins; lunch never less than a couple of courses; and at least once a week dinner was a massive roast. Gourmet pizzas appeared on the weekends.

At the end of a meal, a fancy espresso machine catered for most caffeine tastes. Nothing went to waste: the asparagus left over from one meal would become soup at next day's lunch. It was a mammoth, exhausting juggling act for the two chefs and their kitchen help, but their humour always remained intact. The only time I saw Jeff perturbed was at the sight of a particularly tall bulldozer driver chomping his way through at least six poached eggs one breakfast. Fresh supplies — 'freshies' in base lingo — landed only every two weeks, and at the rate the bulldozer driver was eating there seemed every chance that Jeff would run out of eggs.

We queued up for our first meal — dinner — and settled at one of the long tables. We were trying to get to know each other as much as we were the rest of the base. Vikki and Tania were lecturers from the Christchurch College of Education. Vikki had been planning the trip for some time, but at the last minute her planned team-mate had been unable to come and Tania was the replacement. Tania's late sign-up for the trip only seemed to have heightened her enthusiasm. Vikki and Tania planned to write teaching units on Antarctica for social studies classes that Antarctica New Zealand would be able to add to its website. Chris taught science and outdoor education to student teachers at Wellington College of Education and wanted to use his time on the ice to help persuade his colleagues of the need to link science with other teaching disciplines. He was an outdoors type and stayed determinedly in his salopettes and allocated long-sleeved undergarment for the entire stay.

Lucrezia was also a teacher. This was the first time that an Italian teacher had come on the New Zealand programme. She had, we were told, developed impressive Antarctic teaching resources for her school, but it was hard to find out just what she knew or thought. The shock and duration of her journey from Italy to Antarctica — with virtually no breaks on the way — had robbed her of her scant command of English.

After dinner, the amiable Chet, the base services manager, rounded up the newcomers, the DVs and us. Safe and convivial communal living meant adhering to the rules, he told us. We learnt about signing out in the book down at the office every time we left the base; being late back would trigger a search and rescue call-out. If there was a fire we had to go out the nearest door — some doors had a big drop onto the snow — and assemble by the flag-pole. Even if we were in the shower, as some unlucky souls have been, we had to muster as soon as possible at the flag-pole. On a continent that hoards much of the world's fresh water, fire is one of the biggest hazards. The dry atmosphere and the linked walkways are potential accelerants if any fire gains a foothold. If there was a serious fire — and a British laboratory on the other side of the continent on the Antarctic Peninsula had burnt to the ground

From McMurdo Station, the Ferrar Glacier glistens as it slides towards the sea. On the hill stands Vince's Cross.
PHOTO: CHRIS ARCUS

The day before departure I visit Canterbury Museum to give the proboscis on the bust of Norwegian explorer Roald Amundsen a rub for luck.

On the five-hour flight south, people and cargo are squashed uncomfortably close together.

Togged up in extreme-cold-weather gear, I prepare to embark the Starlifter.

A Starlifter lands on the 2-metre thick sea ice runway. PHOTO: CHRIS ARCUS

The world's most southerly active volcano, Mt Erebus, wreathed with a wisp of cloud.

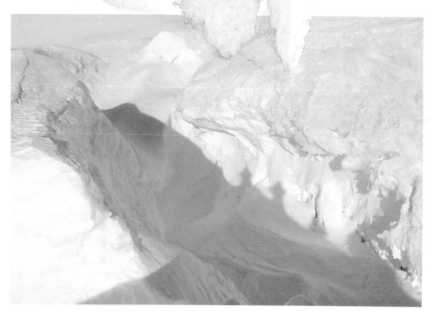

Standing on the edge of this crevasse I peek over to snap my shadow far below.

Constructing the snow mound we are to sleep in during field training is basic but energetic work. PHOTO: CHRIS ARCUS

A pee tent gives a modicu
of privacy, but wiggling
through the opening in
bulky extreme-cold-weather
gear is fraught with
difficulty.
PHOTO: CHRIS ARCUS

Weary builders stand before
the finished snow mound.
We've set up our 'kitchen'
al fresco.
PHOTO: TANIA MCBRIDE/
VIKKI PINK

The sign at 77°51′ South is a popular spot for posed photos.

The array of recycling bins at McMurdo includes one for rubbish for Antarctica's scavenging bird, the skua. PHOTO: CHRIS ARCUS

In the Scott Base's library, Chris, Tania, Vikki and Natalie mull over the day's activities.

The edge of the Barne Glacier looms over those who stop on the way to and from Shackleton's hut.
PHOTO: CHRIS ARCUS

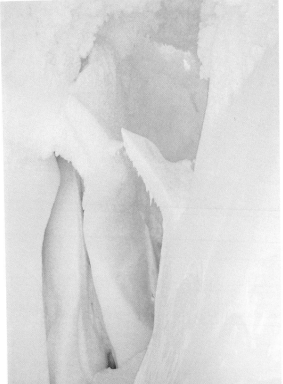

The soaring roof of one of Antarctica's spectacular ice caves.
PHOTO: CHRIS ARCUS

From the polar plateau the ice grinds its way inexorably to the coast, tumbling over the mountains to form a huge frozen waterfall.
PHOTO: CHRIS ARCUS

Through the crackled crust of Lake Vanda we could see algae and white globules of trapped air.
PHOTO: CHRIS ARCUS

the previous month — our refuge would be a small hut separate from the rest of the base, part of the original base and home to Sir Edmund Hillary more than 40 years earlier. Unsurprisingly, smoking was not encouraged. I never figured out who the smokers were; addicts were quarantined in an external hut.

We also had to learn to keep discharging the static electricity that built up in the dry atmosphere by flicking our fingers against the strips of metal that lined the hallway walls and the edges of desks. It had to become second nature. Leaving it to build up could — literally — blow up electrical equipment and give another person a painful shock. But it was fun to allow a little build-up, especially after a hair wash — my fine hair floated mermaid-style around my head.

We were urged to drink often from the large water dispenser in the mess to avoid dehydration, and reminded to watch our urine. When it started to go brown — and that could happen quickly — you needed to drink more. We had to 'conserve water but NOT at the expense of personal hygiene' the Scott Base booklet warned. Going feral was not an option here. Chet also inducted us into the dishwashing routine: if your plates were the last to fill up one of the washing trays, it fell to you to load the tray into the dishwasher. Once I skipped back in the queue, claiming to have forgotten something, when I realised the chore would fall to me, but I felt so guilty that I later unburdened myself to Chet. He chided me gently — 'Ahh, but that's bucking the communal system' — and I didn't shy from the task again.

The briefing had been relaxed but thorough, a hallmark of

all official dealings at the New Zealand base. It was 'She'll be right', but with a caveat: '. . . as long as we make sure it is.' Chet told us we were not to think of ourselves as guests, even though we were only there for just over a week. We were now part of the base, he said, but we knew that you only really become accepted when someone showed you how to use the espresso machine.

Next day was to be field training. Mountaineers Jim and Lisa would take Tania, Vikki, Chris, Marj, Michelle, Lucrezia and I out to learn the rudiments of survival on the ice. We gathered for our briefing in a room in the administration section of the base. The room also doubled as the movie theatre, the only audiovisual entertainment the base provided. I never made it to a movie, but in a too-short week I didn't miss that, or television. Lisa and Jim quickly ran through the elements of the next day and a half's training: we'd learn how to walk on icy slopes, identify a crevasse and build and sleep in a survival snow mound. To Chris, well-versed in the skill of living outdoors, it sounded like fun; to me, it sounded utterly daunting.

More challenging still — the women in the group needed to learn to pee outdoors. Pulling down your salopettes in minus 20 degrees was clearly not an option. Chris and Jim were ushered out of the briefing room while we unwrapped our Freshettes. The pink extension tubes were threaded into the rubbery cups and we all slipped off to the toilets to practise. A half-remembered struggle with my first tampon resurfaced as I tried awkwardly to position the cup in just the right spot before using it. 'You just have to make sure the pipe is pushed

50

down a bit,' I called triumphantly to the others as a yellow stream hit the side of the toilet bowl. Cries of delight in the other stalls followed as Tania and Vikki and the others conquered their Freshettes. This must have been the last straw for Lucrezia; not long after this she retreated to her bed, desperate for sleep.

Later, Natalie took the others for a walk on the sea ice just outside the base. I demurred and spent part of the evening writing. 'You've got to experience things to write about them,' Natalie advised. I would fit everything in, I thought confidently. At midnight I plucked up the courage to have a drink in the bar, but, outside the door, I began to worry that the atmosphere might be too much like a rugby club for comfort. The only time I had ever fitted in with the rugby boys at my school had been completely inadvertent. I transferred from a school that had allowed girls to wear their uniforms short. In my new, more conservatively attired school this was an unintended signal. For a few short months, until I changed into a lower-hemmed gym slip, I had a boyfriend in the First Fifteen.

Through the bar door I spied Tim, a scientist I had met in Wellington, so I went in and asked him how I bought a drink. I'd only met Tim once before, and then only to interview him for a story I was writing, but he greeted me warmly. I was too late to buy myself a drink (the bar closed on weeknights at 10:30 p.m. and 11:30 p.m. on Saturdays), so Tim handed me one of the cans he and his friends had lined up around the wall behind the pool table. The atmosphere was welcoming, but even so I declined the offer of a game of pool and quickly downed my one can of beer. I just couldn't get to grips with having to drink in the bar's broad daylight.

Unable to settle to sleep yet, I wandered through the corridors of the base, trying as I went to remember to discharge the endless static that clung to my body in the arid atmosphere. Each corridor window framed its own masterpiece of mountain, ice and sky, illuminated by the constant bright sunlight. The sun had risen here a week and a half earlier and would not set again for six months. For the length of the austral summer, it would make lazy laps of the southern sky.

At midnight I dragged myself away from the magical view and decided I should go to bed.

It was minus 27 degrees Celsius the first time I stepped outside the base the next morning. Factor in the wind chill and it was minus 41 degrees. My nose hairs froze. For the next day and a half, we were heading out for what's called field training, an odd term to use in a place without a single blade of grass. The aim, although we didn't realise it at once, was to gain some understanding of Antarctica's seductive menace.

Mountaineers Jim and Lisa gathered our group in the field store building to equip us with harnesses and crampons before we left. Lucrezia was still in bed, ill with fatigue, so with Tania, Vikki and Chris, Lisa and our minder Natalie, and Michelle and Marj, I tried to select the right crampons and harnesses for the day's travel over crevasses. I stepped into a harness, a complicated collection of straps and loops designed to ensure we all stayed attached to a rope and each other as we moved over the ice. Being tied together, I was told, would mean that we could be retrieved if we did manage to end up in a crevasse.

With some help from Chris, I managed to adjust the harness comfortably around my waist and legs, but strapping crampons over my fat mukluks seemed impossible. I worried that the pair I'd chosen and managed to attach was only just gripping the toes of my boots. I had no idea what I was doing.

Before we left, we had to learn how to work the primus provided in the survival bags carried by every field trip. It seemed an awkward combination of methylated spirits and kerosene, but in the cold it was the only way to rustle up a flame. The design is little changed from that used by the explorers in the first Antarctic huts almost a hundred years ago. It had played a vital part in the Antarctica story as, without it, no one could ever have countenanced leaving the coast. I mused about writing a new niche history entitled *The Primus Stove and How It Changed the World* but abandoned my reverie when it was my turn to struggle to make the primus light.

There was a load of gear to pack into our transport, which was a cross between a truck and a bulldozer, called a Nodwell. Food came in a red box, kitchen utensils in yellow and the primus gear in blue. If you forgot which was which, you could always refer to Antarctica New Zealand's field manual. All the organisational wisdom distilled from a century of Antarctic exploring had been crammed into this compact book. I had grabbed one back in New Zealand when I got my clothing. It covered everything you needed to know about travelling and surviving in the local terrain. There was even a guide to the ideal layout of equipment in the pyramid polar tent, the modern-day descendant of the tents the first Antarcticans used.

After loading the Nodwell with food, sleeping bags, mats and other safety gear, including those wretched crampons, we clambered into its windowless passenger cabin and sat waiting while Lisa and Jim tried to rouse the reluctant motor. It was apparently reticent because of the cold. We understood, particularly when we could spend this welcome delay back in the mess eating Jeff's delicious cinnamon scones.

But a delay is all it was: no first-time visitor to New Zealand's part of Antarctica escapes field training. 'It's really to give newcomers a taste of real Antarctica, because it's too easy to step inside the building and think, 'Oh yeah, I've done Antarctica,' Lisa explained later. As we finally left, I regretted having only one scone.

Reconciled to the cold, the Nodwell lumbered around a small corner of the Ross Ice Shelf in the direction of the training area. Tonight we would sleep on a slab of ice the size of France. Tucked away in the back it was hard to tell exactly where we were going with just the bumpy swish of the back of the truck to guide us, but it wasn't long before we had stopped beside an icy slope. Here we would learn how to chop steps into a slope and use an ice axe to stop ourselves from slipping. As we twisted our mukluks into our crampons, the snow squeaked under our feet. It was so dry that it felt like some sort of coarse sugar; the snowballs we attempted to make just crumbled in our hands. We weren't allowed to dally long, though. We were behind schedule, which is never a good place to be in the structured life of Antarctica. I advanced tentatively up the slope.

The first lesson was cutting steps out of the side of the hill.

Though he had seemed awkward, in that tall person's way, back at Scott Base, here Jim snapped on his sunglasses and seemed to meld right into the slope. Jim swung his axe expertly and we followed. We had to build several before trying to step up the slope. My legs seemed rooted to the ice, but Jim patiently prised me out. The instructor's hearts must sink every time they encounter a nervous beginner like me, but they were impeccably professional and any such feelings never showed on their patient, friendly faces.

With our tentative steps cut and climbed, Jim and Lisa split the group into two to teach us how to stop ourselves from sliding down an icy slope. The technique of 'self arresting' without an ice axe involved rolling over onto our fronts and pushing ourselves up with our arms so our feet dug in. Then we learnt to stop ourselves sliding down the mountain by slapping an ice axe into the slope. Once I'd figured out how to hold the axe so as not to impale myself, I began to enjoy the exercise. Next we were all tethered together to walk up the hill to a crevasse field. Leading the way was Lisa, her body enviably taut and her face buffed glowingly smooth by the elements. 'I bet she's done a few 8000-metre peaks,' said Chris admiringly.

Walking up an ice slope tethered together was much, much harder than I anticipated. My feet slipped inside the mukluks, and my crampons seemed loose. We stopped while Jim checked my feet, and everyone waited patiently as I was moved to the position just behind Lisa. Her calm, soothing voice urged me to find a slow, steady rhythm, and I began to feel more in control. I knew my body was unlikely to serve me well in the

Antarctic, but it wasn't as if I hadn't trained for this. Unfortunately, it seemed that my suburban perambulations had been a somewhat inadequate preparation.

I managed to stumble up the slope and we set off across a seemingly flat piece of snow — one that was riddled with crevasses. The aim was to instil in us a healthy aversion to deviating from the flagged routes. Two Americans did that once, after taking a short cut home across benign-looking snow after discovering they were late for the McMurdo dinner. In the frozen belly of the hidden crevasse they fell into, one died immediately; the other lived, they think, for about half an hour.

Lisa led us across a series of stable snow bridges, then we had to cross one that was not solid at all. 'Just take an easy stride,' Lisa commanded. I did, edging tentatively forward towards the gaping wound of a crevasse. Lisa gracefully pulled her roped-up charges in towards her and we all peered down into the void. My shadow captured deep in the crevasse's blue maw is the only photographic evidence that I was ever there; I was too afraid to move enough to hand my camera over to anyone else.

The DVs had a simpler version of our field training: a stroll over sea ice and a briefing back at Scott Base. I later railed to Chris against the injustice of spending a precious day and a half of our trip doing field training, but he was having none of my impatience. 'How else could we learn, except by doing?' he asked. And he was right: even my painful mukluk lesson was valuable. It was all about learning just what your equipment did, Jim reassured me, even down to the smallest item. 'What you know in New Zealand is useful, but when you get down here it's actually which pair of gloves do you want to work in? Which pair of pants do you want to work in?' It seemed incongruous in all this grandeur to be worrying about which gloves to wear, but that was precisely the point. If you let the landscape overwhelm you, survival became a tenuous thing.

As we edged away from the crevasse, we were able to take in the panorama. We had travelled down the other side of the arm of Ross Island on which Scott Base was perched and there behind us was Mt Erebus. It was the first time we'd seen its full outline. It was an awesome view in all senses of the word. (It also began to seem much more apt that one of Ross Island's other mountains was named Mt Terror.) I had handled a piece of lava from Mt Erebus during my study at university. That innocuous piece of scratchy rock, little different from any other I had handled in the volcanic countryside surrounding my childhood home town, had been collected by a New Zealand geologist. He had been on the side of Erebus when the mountain had spat this out at his feet.

Returning down the slope seemed much easier, and the crevasses more manageable. Towards the end we even managed a faster pace. I allowed myself a small grin of success. As we climbed back into the Nodwell for another bumpy ride where we would sleep that night, Lisa told me I had my hat on inside out.

The remnants of the shelters of those who came before us made a ruined crystal city at the snow mound site. After a little preamble from Jim on technique, we piled our sleeping bags and mats onto the snow. We were to learn not so much the art of making a snow mound, but the slog. There were three labouring jobs: shovelling the snow into a mound; quarrying snow from the edge of the ditch that grows around the mound; and patting the dome smooth. We took turns at all three, with the very fit Jim and Lisa helping, speeding up what seemed like an endless process. The slapping of our shovels onto the snow to pack it down was soon the only sound in the sunlit Antarctic landscape. 'This is installation art,' said Chris dreamily. It took most of the afternoon and some of the putative night to build the mound in which we would sleep.

Lunch was the cheese and pickle sandwiches we'd prepared before we left base, and extra muesli bars for afters. The sandwiches were frozen. For Lisa and Jim, this was apparently nothing out of the ordinary (I doubted that anything in this landscape was for them). I forced myself to chew through the frozen food. There was no choice, as here sustenance really does sustain you. On this trip, Natalie introduced me to hot Raro, a powdered orange-flavoured juice in boiling water. At home I wouldn't have touched this strange drink; here I became a committed fan. In the distance we could see our first Antarctic mirage, a hazy simmering slab that boosted a faraway cliff well above its true height. The old explorers made up words for the strange wonders the ice conjures up: 'ice blink' and 'water sky' were two favourites from the dictionary I had of Antarctic English (I had bought it before I left and lugged it down to the ice). I had been comforted to read, back in my safe and cosy suburb, that the word 'tea bag' had its origins on the ice. Using a cloth bag to enclose tea leaves was, the dictionary said, an Antarctic invention. On early expeditions, tea bags were scavenged from rubbish dumps and often used several times. At times of desperation, they were even smoked.

The mound finally reached a height approved by Jim — high enough not to collapse in the night and bury us. Our six-person home for the night was completed by hollowing out two entrances, then dragging out the snow inside along with the buried gear. The mound complete, it was time to brave the toilet. The toilet was a bucket, set up inside a tent. The tent was pyramid-shaped to withstand the onslaught of Antarctic blizzards and to keep the snow out it had an entrance like a vacuum cleaner pipe about a foot or so off the ground. The bucket, with a small seat across it, was at the far side of the tent, out of reach of blundering newcomers as they wriggled through the entrance. The bucket's contents were frozen, but that did nothing to stop the stink. I wriggled in and out of my gear as quickly as I could.

To graduate from field training we had to survive making our dinner and sleeping in the snow mound on our own. The instructors and Natalie were to sleep nearby in the heated comfort of a small A-frame hut. We were not allowed, we were told sternly, to even consider sleeping in a supplies hut near our snow mound. Then they fired up the Nodwell and left.

Left to ourselves, we propped two primus stoves onto a shelf of ice, out of a zephyr of wind. It took us several attempts to light the stoves, but we soon had pots of snow set on top.

Our food preparation was not particularly complex: all we had to do was to add hot water to the selection of dehydrated meals from our food box. Bringing ice to the boil took an age, however. As we waited, we women spent time bemoaning the state of our hair, the only distinctive thing showing above our blue layers. I had briefly removed my hat and the moisture in my hair had frozen. It looked like hoar frost; the fine blonde hair of another woman in our team had turned into spun sugar. Tania's carefully streaked and moussed hair had been flattened by the dry atmosphere and her hat. 'Aargh,' said Tania, feeling her straightened hair, 'that's not a good look.'

The wind was whipping up to blow snaking lines of snow across the ice towards us. Even dressed in extreme-cold-weather clothing, the cold seeped through. The remedy was a brisk walk around a track made by the Nodwell. Michelle and I split off and soon found that the simple mechanism of plodding around the track was restoring warmth to our bodies. I felt trapped: despite the vast ice shelf stretching out before us we were confined to our mound (even the remnants of other mounds were out of bounds, in case they collapsed) and the track. But the isolation of 'survival camp' was a mirage; later on that night, a couple of people skied out for exercise from Scott Base.

When the water finally deigned to boil, we divvied it up for the bags of food. We had to keep the bags upright while the water rehydrated the food. It was hard to be patient: the effort of building the mound and the cold meant we were longing for food. In the old days, they ate 'hoosh' when they were 'in the field'. Hoosh was a hot soupy stew of pemmican

60

(dried and crushed meat), with biscuits or oatmeal added for thickening. After a hard day's sledging, I imagine anything would have tasted good. One of the hardiest of the explorers, Thomas Crean, once drank boiling curry, after the powder was mixed with hot water by mistake, instead of cocoa. He drank it without complaint. The water had barely boiled when I added the hard ingredients of my seafood-flavoured bag, and the bits of food had barely rehydrated when I ate the contents as fast as I could.

It was late by the time we all crawled into our snow mound. We'd dithered over how everyone would fit in: Chris, the tallest, ended up along the length of the mound and the rest of us slept at right angles to him. Michelle lay beside me and Marj, Vikki and Tania were at the other end. As we each crawled into our allotted slot, we took off a very few layers of clothing and squirmed into the two sleeping bags each person had been allocated. Outside the wind had lowered the temperature to about minus 40 degrees.

Scott's companions, Aspley Cherry-Garrard, Bill Wilson and Birdie Bowers, had been connoisseurs of cold. They spent a week in winter traversing Ross Island in search of emperor penguin eggs, discussing whether the minus 54 degrees weather was a cold snap and what, indeed, constituted a cold snap. As I lay next to Michelle, trying to get comfortable enough to sleep, I realised I wasn't the only one that was finding the going tough. Michelle was relieving her feelings by cursing her boss, the head of Antarctica New Zealand. 'Feckin' Gill, why did she feckin' want me to do this?' Tania started to complain loudly that someone had the most incredible wind.

Apparently the dehydrated food was to blame. Tania and Vikki tried to ferret out the source, but no one owned up.

I shivered quietly and asked Chris if this experience was likely to be life threatening. He said it wasn't so I tried to sleep. The early explorers regularly woke up with reindeer hair from their bags in their mouths. They endured, and I reminded myself that they would probably have enjoyed what we were doing. I pulled the hood of the sleeping bag over my head to block out the light from the sun, and for the first time in years I felt desperately homesick.

Getting up in the morning took us an hour and a half. One by one, we had to sit up, reapply our layers of clothing, and then crawl backwards out of the mound. We hauled out our sleeping gear, packed it back into the bags, and then tried to rustle up the energy to have breakfast — a hot Raro and a muesli bar. Lisa, Jim and Natalie came back from their heated hut to get us. Apparently some people had told them in the past that it was the best sleep they'd had in years. We all agreed that our rest had been varied at best. Marj, the light sleeper, looked haggard. 'At least you slept,' she said, darting a look my way. I was hungry, cold and sulky. I couldn't help what happened when I was asleep. At least I wasn't the one with wind, I thought to myself. In the back of the truck, at the insistence of the hardy Tania, we propped up the full toilet bucket, trying to ensure the frozen contents did not fall out on the bumpy drive back to base.

The welcoming green of Scott Base's buildings was tantalisingly close but our field training was not yet over. First we had to march out onto the sea ice. In summer this stretch would sometimes become open water. In the Transantarctic Expedition hut hung a photo of a minke whale cruising just off the beach at Pram Point. Pram, it turned out, had its place in Antarctic history: it was Scott who named the New Zealand beach, because he had explored it in a pram, which was the name for a Norwegian-style dinghy.

To check the thickness of sea ice, travellers still use a traditional ice auger — 'a bloody great corkscrew and a tape measure', Lisa called it. In the unforgiving Antarctic landscape, it pays to stick to tried-and-true methods. We took turns to whirl an auger into the ice, and watched as McMurdo Sound spurted up in answer. It seemed there were just a couple of metres between us and the water. A seal hole was nearby; Lisa poked it with a stick to encourage the seal to leap up, but I only saw its nose. It hissed at us as it gulped some air. We were warned not to get too close to seals — they could be aggressive, especially if there were pups around. And, of course, we were warned not to fall in. The lack of contour here was deceptive. 'What do you think you are standing on, Kim?' asked Jim languidly. I looked down at the smooth slice of snow below me and hastily jumped aside from the snow bridge, hiding a crevasse, that was taking my weight — for now.

Our last stop was the huge hangar housing the field stores where we had started a long day and a half ago. Here we had to learn to put together the tent that could save our lives in a blizzard. Even if we were in a Nodwell, Lisa told us, the tent had to go up. The cosy warmth of a vehicle soon dissipated once it had stopped and it became a refrigerator.

'If there's no wind, which way should you orient the back

of the tent?' asked Lisa. My diligence in meteorology would pay off at last: 'South,' I said, 'because of the katabatic winds.' 'Right,' said Lisa, looking somewhat startled by this unexpected display of knowledge. So our small group wrestled with the two-person tent, a tiny version of the elongated field huts we would see later. Finally, we were allowed to leave the hangar and walk through the brilliant sunshine to the warmth of the base. The chances of having to use our survival lessons in earnest seemed remote, but even the magnificent Lisa was wary of Antarctica. 'Every time I pack my sack to go out, I put the extras in, thinking, I know the weather's good but it could be one of those days coming out to bite you.'

A group that followed us the next week were out for a walk on the sea ice when a blizzard descended. They radioed for help and Lisa, having a meal at the base, had to tog up to go and find them. They were, in fact, just outside the base, near one of the buildings, completely unable to see their way home in the Antarctic squall.

Civilisation

3

and here we are
with our
thousand footsteps
etcetera
Some Frames – Bill Manhire

I FLIPPED OPEN THE HANDLE ON THE THICK DOOR THAT KEPT THE heat sealed into the squat green buildings. They were, in essence, freezers, except that here, of course, they were keeping the heat in. It was a relief to shed my outdoors layers; the hot water in the shower made my chilled skin tingle.

In the mess, I wolfed down at least two helpings of the lunch that had been saved for us. Mealtimes were my chance to mix with the staff at the base. I was their first journalist of the season. The year before, one reporter who made the journey south had written about how people at the base manage for sex. The standard code for 'Do not disturb', he wrote, was to leave one shoe, instead of two, outside a closed bunkroom door. The staff on the base had been warned not to titillate the journalists passing through this year, and I never did find out if the shoe story was true. Probably to head off any similar stories, Gill Wratt, the head of Antarctica New Zealand had barely introduced herself to me before I was gently scolded. I had written an article before I left describing Antarctic workers as predominantly male, bearded, fascinated by rocks, ice and strange microorganisms. 'As you can see, that's not the case,' said Gill crisply, gesturing around at the eclectic mix of people in the dining room.

The people at Scott Base, both workers and visitors, did tend to challenge my preconceptions. Each summer, a team of 30 staff kept the base running. Keith and Annette were one of the two married couples on the base. The hardest part of spending time in Antarctica for Annette was being away from her four-year-old grandson. Keith, or Grumps as he was called, policed the telephones. Infringements — blowing up the phones with static electricity was one of the worst crimes — were written into a notebook housed in Keith's pocket. At the weekly base meetings, miscreants were cheerfully denounced.

Along with Annette, who worked in the kitchen and was the qualified first aider, Keith would stay on for the winter. 'Our children don't worry about it. We've just gone to work. We'll come home in a year. It's a very long workday as far as they are concerned,' Annette told me. For Keith it was his third full year in Antarctica (with breaks in between): routine was the key, he confided. During each stint on the ice, he had called his family on Wednesdays or Saturdays and washed his clothes on Sundays.

Having married couples on the base — and a mix of ages — created a more normal living environment, according to the eminently sensible Gill, who quickly dismissed any ideas I might have had that the New Zealand base was some kind of libidinous playground. The machines stocked with chocolate, strawberry and mint-flavoured condoms in the staff toilets were merely a practical response to the base's isolation, she told me. 'It's part of our responsibility in running an isolated base where people can't just go down to a shop for what they need, as they would back home.' All field parties, Marj told me, were supplied with condoms. Over at McMurdo, the Americans have had condoms on offer for years. Sara Wheeler, in her book *Terra Incognita*, records their usefulness in keeping the wind off her microphone. Anyway, Gill needn't have worried about my writing salacious stories. I had my own built-in deterrent. My daily online stories were soon printed out and clipped to the base noticeboard in the mess; that previous reporter had been far away from Scott Base by the time his story made it into print.

Scott Base offered plenty of other energetic outlets for excess energy. One of the container buildings housed a small gym (I never ventured there); there were regular sporting competitions with neighbouring base McMurdo (New Zealand always wins at rugby); cross-country skiing (Chris slipped fearlessly across the sea ice in minus 29 degrees Celsius one evening); and mountain bikes. The base even boasted a rudimentary downhill ski slope. As we toured the base after recovering from our field training, we saw the engine of an old army truck having hot air being blown into it, like a sort of huge vacuum cleaner in reverse. Dormant all winter, the engine was being warmed up for the ski season, 'opening' in a couple of weeks, when the truck would serve as the Scott Base Ski Club's ski tow. So dry was the snow, the downhill skiers had to wait for the warmer summer weather to begin.

As a 20-year-old university student, a Scott Base summer job had seemed like a dream: an exotic location, money and nothing much to spend it on. I imagined it being like a Club Med organiser, except at the other temperature extreme. In fact, everyone — from the cleaners to the mechanics — worked very hard. Cath, one of the domestics, was constantly gliding around the hallways, mopping as she listened to music through her headphones. She and her companion cleaner, Helen, alternated their duties, in order to keep their interest up. The base was never less than sparkling after all their gliding and gilding. Whenever I passed Cath, a serene smile appeared on her face. I guessed the banality and repetition of the job was offset by the weekends. On Sunday she strapped on cross-country skis and followed the sea ice road around the coast of Ross Island as far as Cape Evans.

Touring the base was a relaxing change after the arduous start to our week, not least because the internal air temperature was constant at a pleasant 20 degrees Celsius. That was the responsibility of the engineering group, who numbered eight in summer and five in the winter, the largest group on the base. Alan, the engineering manager, was a clever, handsome young man who had left a fiancée behind in Christchurch. He entertained us with complicated explanations of how the salt water sucked out of the Ross Sea was transformed into our drinking water. Inside the base we saw machinery that filled a room — all for extracting the salt from the sea water, not once, but twice. At Scott Base, he told us, the water was much cleaner than the World Health Organisation's minimum standard. We were relieved to have had this explanation once we went outside on the tour and saw that the pipe that sucked the sea water out seemed to be awfully close to the one transporting waste out to sea.

Alan leant against the pipe spitting grey waste water and worse into the sea and explained how the waste was macerated before spilling. The solid trail of brown, snap-frozen between the pipe and the sea, was testament to his words. The winter job for the engineers was to install a sewage treatment plant to ensure the area's environmental sanctity was restored. Though the macerated waste was still acceptable under the environmental rules of the Antarctic, Antarctica New Zealand had decided that spilling raw sewage into Antarctic waters could no longer be condoned. The new system would be a far cry from one picture I had seen during my course at the university. It showed the RBT glacier, named for the long-time Antarctic manager (he of the lime green buildings), and consisting of a frozen pile of waste that had spewed out of a pipe and onto the ice. I edged closer to the end of the pipe to get a photograph. The Antarctic dictionary didn't list the word, but I had been told, straight-faced, that the shards of brown ice were known as shit-sicles. Someone flushed the toilet on base. We all jumped back from the pipe.

Around the back of the base, Alan enticed Vikki, Tania and Chris up onto the water tanks. It was, he promised, a fantastic view. The tanks, flat-topped, with no railing, looked too slippery for safety and I hung around the bottom while the others nimbly climbed up to peer into the distance. It was thanks to these tanks that we were allowed such liberality in our showers at Scott Base; apparently, constant demand kept the water in motion and prevented it from freezing into rotund ice blocks.

Prowling around nearby were the bulldozers. They were used to keep the constantly encroaching ice and snow at bay. Too much build-up could eventually damage the structure of the buildings. I waved to one of the drivers, the man whose appetite had threatened the chef's egg supply.

Back inside, we visited the hydroponics room, a warm, brightly lit room devoted to growing plants. Ample bushes dotted with chilli peppers and zucchinis were growing rampantly up wire netting. Other plants — cucumbers, capsicums, tomatoes and lettuces — were also raised to add to the already varied diet for the summer. In winter, they provided much-needed fresh food. With its flowing-water sound effects and moisture-laden air, the room provided a gentle touch of home, and it was the only place where greenery scented the air. 'We are actually toying with the idea of putting a hammock in here,' our guide told us. I learnt later that two Kiwis had posed in McMurdo's hydroponics room as part of New Zealand's contribution to an unusual Antarctic calendar. Instead of the regulation penguins and icebergs, the calendar starred nude locals, posing in Antarctic settings. The New Zealanders used hydroponic greenery for modesty. All 500 copies of the 2000 calendar entitled 'Welcome to the Bottom of Our World', sold out in two days.

The base had a food freezer in one of its container buildings. The food had to be kept frozen, but not at the low level of the outside air. A separate warm store, set at about the temperature of a domestic refrigerator, stored food such as potatoes, jams and cheeses. Jeff and Clare carefully guarded the kitchen rations to ensure adequate supplies, but for those in the know — and Tania and Vikki later confessed that they had raided the secret supply of chocolate pinwheel scones — there were hidden delicacies.

Official hours of work at the base were from 8 a.m. until 5 p.m., but many had to work whenever a problem presented itself, and the stress of work sometimes took its toll. The last time I saw Alan the engineer it was early in the morning and he was fixing something to do with the toilets. I heard later that he had returned to New Zealand early. Maybe the endless hours of work had just been too much. The budget for the entire support operation was just $6 million — not much more than the annual budget of a medium to large New Zealand high school, Chris pointed out. The next year, Antarctica New Zealand argued its cause for more money and the New Zealand government allocated them another million.

Juggling roles must have been the hardest thing for the Scott Base staff; their role was to keep the base working perfectly as a constant stream of visitors passed through, many keen to party. The notes for Scott Base newbies had warned me that a costume for Halloween was a must. (For toga parties it seemed that bring your own sheets from New Zealand was the rule: using sheets from the base for toga costumes would annoy the domestic staff.) So, before I left home, I headed to the wackiest costume-hire place in town, where the madly enthusiastic owner rummaged through many aisles to find me what I wanted. Fantasy was to be my theme, I'd decided. After all, I came from the country that had given filmic life to J.R.R. Tolkien's Middle Earth. And, being short of stature, with brown wavy hair, what else could I be than a hobbit. After much rummaging, I left the costume shop slightly embarrassed, but triumphant. My bag was stuffed with fake pointy ears, a dirndl skirt, a green braid-trimmed apron, and a puffy-sleeved white blouse. I had asked a one-time *The Lord of the Rings* extra to tell me just what 40-something female hobbits wore and this seemed close enough to pass muster. My mukluks would make perfect feet, I decided, with the additional inelegance of stockings pulled over them.

Sadly, I was too late for the official Halloween party at McMurdo. The Americans only allowed serious carousing on a Saturday. On the actual night of Halloween, the Wednesday we were there, anyone who turned up to a trivia contest at McMurdo wearing a costume was offered a prize. But I felt too shy to parade my hobbit gear in the bright lights of the cavernous American mess. I left it stuffed into a corner of my green holdall. If I had gone, I felt certain that someone would have asked me to yodel.

There were no such constraints on weeknight parties at the New Zealand base (although the loudest volume notch on the ancient stereo in the mess had been fixed about two-thirds of the way around the dial). The constant ebb and flow of people at the base encouraged a convivial atmosphere and the ties back to our New Zealand lives were loosened.

At Scott Base the bar was the social focus. During the day, the bar was a comfortable place to curl up with a book; during the evening hours, the constant daylight meant that the bleary traces of alcohol were only too evident. Thursday nights were American nights, the one night a week that the New Zealanders allowed the locals from the far more populous McMurdo to flood into the bar. The 80-cent cans of beer at the Kiwi bar were an enormous lure. I poked my head around the door on the Thursday I was there. The bar was packed and, though I spied the nurse who had been opposite me on the plane, I decided not to hang about.

Before they left, the Distinguished Visitors (they were heading back a couple of days earlier than us) invoked a base tradition by putting on caps before they wandered in. Wearing hats in the bar meant they had to throw some of their not inconsiderable wealth into the bar's tambourine, the receptacle for donations towards drinks. Late in the evening, I came into the bar to wish them well before the journey home. 'Are we on the record?' one of them immediately asked. They probably had good reason to be wary of the media, though I had only wanted to say goodbye. Still, it seemed fair enough that even DVs should be allowed to let their hair down a little and it was probably easier without a journalist around. I went to bed early, at midnight.

The next day the New Zealand flag was flapping loose

from its flag-pole. Apparently, during the night someone had decided to try to change the New Zealand flag for the corporate flag of the business of one of the DVs. The next morning, everyone just carried on, complicit in their camaraderie.

Travelling around the hill to the — by Antarctic standards — huge American base felt strange. I was reminded of the time I flew from Tokyo to London via Anchorage. The Alaskan airport was a discordant hiatus between the two tradition-bound cultures where I made my home for a few years each. The airport lounge had a spectacular vista of mountains that, after the chaos of Tokyo, seemed almost surreal. In Japan I drank green tea; in London I would learn to drink my tea very brown. Here I sipped weak black tea with lemon, trying to decipher the cacophony of voices around me. McMurdo, too, seemed harsh after the cosiness of the Kiwi base. For Tania, it recalled an ugly town she had seen in northern Japan. There were mud-brown, multi-storey dormitories and a sprawling laboratory that seemed to slide down the entire side of one hill. The whole place was cobwebbed with overhead wires and the roads were a slushy, grainy brown from constant use. Outside the dormitories were colour-coded rubbish bins: some for plastic, some for paper, even one marked for scraps to feed the only flying birds we saw on the ice, the skuas, Antarctica's scavengers. For Chris, a father of three boys, it was the American vehicles that caught his eye. Like everything else at McMurdo, they were huge. 'It's a petrol head's paradise,' said Chris, indulging the masculine interests he had had to suppress all week.

The most beautiful building at McMurdo was the church — the Chapel of the Snows — the only known house of worship on the continent and the most southerly church in the world. The little wooden building perched at the edge of the town had been built using leftovers when McMurdo was first established; there have been various versions since. This latest one was painted white and blue, echoing its surroundings. When we pushed inside, there was a study group there, who graciously beckoned us in to look around. The World Trade Center towers in the US had fallen just six weeks earlier; this small wooden building had been well-used in the ensuing weeks. The window behind the altar looked out over the strip of mountains that had dazzled me on the first day. In the sunshine, through the window of the Chapel of the Snows, we could see blindingly bright glaciers curving around virtually every peak, torrents of ice that came all the way from the polar plateau. The sky sported layer upon layer of blue, as if a painter had been toying with different shades, finally managing to get the sky just right. Brushed across the tops of the mountains, the darkest blue seemed to seep into the distant ice.

The main building, called just Building 155, housed a shop, the galley — as they called their eating hall — and various administrative offices. Natalie directed us to hang our cold-weather gear in one of the many storage bays available outside the shop. The space, after the cramped entranceway at Scott Base, was unnerving. It was important, Natalie warned us, to remember where you had put your jacket. Apparently they were collectors' items. The American jackets were mainly red, unless you did a manual job, in which case you wore brown dungarees. People heading to the South Pole were outfitted in green. Sleekest of them all, everyone agreed, were the jumpsuits worn by the Italians, who passed through each summer on their way to their base at Terra Nova Bay. But, if people at McMurdo wanted to do something out-of-bounds or vaguely naughty, the preferred disguise was a Kiwi's blue jacket. Everyone called the American settlement MacTown and soon, without feeling awkward, we did too.

Despite the external ugliness of MacTown, it was easy to warm to the friendly people who lived there. Science lectures were held at McMurdo twice a week — an Antarctic tradition, harking all the way back to Scott. Virtually everyone from Scott Base went; New Zealanders were invited to all the McMurdo events, as it was easy for the big base to absorb the extras. The Sunday night lecture that week was about underwater camera technology, and when the lights dimmed our lecturer showed us how they had attached the cameras to Weddell seals in Antarctica.

When the lights came up again, I realised with surprise that the tall, blond American who helped run the lecture was someone I'd seen before. Before I left, I had interviewed the McMurdo recreation manager by phone for a story about the American base's annual music festival. He had sent photos and I realised that this was the same guy. I introduced myself and Bill was warmly welcoming, making me regret not getting in touch earlier in my all too short week. The next time we were at McMurdo, Bill spotted me and called out my name. Being recognised made me realise that, in my own transitory way, I was becoming part of the community.

The Kiwis also came to McMurdo to party. That Saturday night, Tania, Vikki and I and some others from the base decided to brave one of the theme parties at the bar called Gallagher's. Jane, who ran the Scott Base shop, was the only one in the requisite Lurex, underneath her jacket. Her resourcefulness was as impressive as her always sleek blonde bob. The rest of us had spruced ourselves up as best we could, and for once we had rebelled against the amorphous extreme-cold-weather gear. However, we couldn't shed them entirely; our evening bags were our green holdalls stuffed with the remaining layers of our cold-weather gear.

On arrival we hung around outside on the steps in the broad daylight. I felt like an awkward teenager, about to enter a party I wasn't really invited to. Inside, the empty dance floor looked as uninviting as the bare hall of any school ball back home. Gallagher's was not my style. With its garish lighting, and some of its male occupants apparently already the worse for wear, it reminded me of very bad public bars in New Zealand. I decided to opt for a glass of New Zealand red wine in more muted company at the Coffee House. It set me back $US3.00.

The Coffee House was in one of the oldest huts at McMurdo — a relic of the Korean War. Inside, the décor was 1970s brown, but I sat enchanted, chatting to the barman (despite its name, the Coffee House did serve alcohol) and my neighbours. For the first time, I felt I could really relax, tucked inside, away from the constant briefings and the demands of my laptop. All too soon, though, our driver insisted on leaving.

If we didn't radio in, he reminded us, we would spark a search and rescue alert. The one night Chris had forgotten to sign in, the person on night-time checks, the 'house mouse', came to make sure he was in his bunk. Tania and Vikki and the others, who had decided to give the disco more of a chance than I did, opted to make the easy 45-minute walk back to Scott Base later. Tiredness was never an issue for serious partygoers; it was just a matter of stepping out into the midnight sun to revive.

I was sorry that I wasn't going to be around for the festival that took place every New Year's Day. Apparently Icestock was the 1990 brainchild of a construction labourer from Iowa. Dane Terry, who helped to run and played in the early Icestock concerts, told me that the labourer's small home town held an annual outdoor music festival they called Cornstock, as a local homage to the seminal 60s festival, Woodstock. So Woodstock begat Cornstock, which eventually begat McMurdo's Icestock. Each year a temporary stage is built, typically a pair of flat-bed trailers from the back of tractors. On top is perched part of an old military accommodation building, providing protection from the wind. Even though it is held in the middle of the Antarctic summer, it is, of course, still a cold gig. Guitars fall out of tune quickly here, because the temperature contracts the metal strings. Players' fingers — and drummers' feet — had been known to freeze. Some years Kiwis have been part of the performance, offering probably the southernmost public performance of the haka. According to Dane, 'The real entertainment value came from the heroics involved with just being there, for bands and audience alike.' The summer I was there the New Year bands ranged from Safety Second to Coldfinger. And, by Antarctic standards, it was T-shirt weather. At the end of the first year of the 21st century, the bands played in a balmy 10 degrees Celsius (51^0F) — a record high for McMurdo.

I rarely looked at the photo of my family on the too-high filing cabinet that was the bedside table. I called the girls in the first few days to reassure them that I was okay, but, as the days wore on, I found it hard to connect with their happy chatter about school and ballet. Their detailed explanations of the latest playground upset washed over me, and I started cutting the conversations short. 'Put me onto Daddy now,' I'd say as some long story rambled out of control. Even my initial unwarranted concern over whether Simon and my mother-in-law would be able to manage all the details of my daughters' busy lives waned.

At first I checked to make sure that Simon had it all straight (we used the computer to chat late at night: a friend had loaded my computer with a programme that allowed me to send messages instantaneously), but eventually tiredness and distance overcame my zeal. Eventually I could only manage desultory remarks: 'Yes, I'm fine.' 'Yes, I'm coping with the cold.' I confided this apparent loss of familial affection to Vikki, but she reassured me it was okay. Our senses were too overloaded, she said, to allow domestic concerns to make their claim.

An unexpected bonus of the trip to Antarctica has been the close bonds that have formed between a trio of teachers

— Tania, Vikki and Chris — and me. We suffered all manner of adversity together, from the field training to the constant briefings. Chris now needed little prompting to help heave me into the back of a ute. Lucrezia occasionally entered the fray, but the language barrier seemed pretty insurmountable.

As the three New Zealand women in the group, Tania, Vikki and I bonded when we were allocated our base chore (everyone got one at the weekly base meetings). We got the task of tying new flags onto bamboo poles. Black flags signified danger and red flags safety. Yellow were used as 'pee poles'; yellow snow was to be avoided. It was important that the bits of cloth didn't rip off in the wind, and ensuring the rectangles of cloth were tight enough to stay secure was a slow process in the freezing hangar. Occasionally we slipped our gloves off for a better grip, but soon stuffed our numbed digits back into their covers.

We used the time to purge ourselves of the niggling frustrations of communal living. Even over a week, a small slight could take on larger proportions. My jarring note had been one person's slightly supercilious air. This person, who probably didn't even realise she'd offended me, had travelled with her family to some exotic places and this, she told me, had inspired her to come to Antarctica to work. I confided my dream of taking my children hiking in the mountains of Bhutan. 'I'm sure you'll be able to travel one day,' she murmured. I longed at that moment to slough off my suburban markings, which were clearly far too obvious. Didn't she realise, I thought indignantly, that I was a well-travelled cosmopolitan, at ease in the liminal space of international airports? Cantabrians Tania and Vikki listened patiently to my moaning, but they had more practical concerns. They took one red and one black flag back to the bar that night to support their home-town rugby team. Tania insisted that they allow her to pin the flags above the bar.

Later that evening, after dinner, we amused ourselves by choosing words from the Antarctic dictionary and trying to guess their meaning. The word yikla took our fancy. It was, the dictionary said, an expression once used by the Australian Antarctic Division in telex transmissions. According to Antarctic lexicographer Bernadette Hince, in the days of limited telex transmissions between the Antarctic bases and Australia, set phrases were represented by combinations of five letters. Yikla meant 'This is the life', and it became our exuberant toast. This increasingly rowdy friendship was somewhat at odds with the usual quiet communal living of an Antarctic base. Noise, it seemed, was confined to the bar. Other areas had to be oases of calm. By the time our final night rolled round, just seven days after we met, we could have gone into the trenches together.

It was probably a good thing for Scott Base we were only there for a week.

4
Heroes

Each man feels as a weight
His own ambition rendered void
Piloting – Chris Orsman

IT HAD BEEN EASY BACK IN WELLINGTON TO ADD TO MY APPLICATION
the promise of a story on the heroic age of Antarctic
exploration. I had cribbed the title, *Made Weak by Time and
Fate*, from the penultimate line of Tennyson's poem 'Ulysses'.
My glib story idea had been to end with a disapproving coda
about the impact of tourists on the huts left behind by the
early explorers; now I was desperate to be one of those tourists.

The itinerary sent to me back in July had said we would be
heading up the coast of Ross Island to Cape Evans and Cape
Royds, the day after our field training. There were three huts

83

from the so-called Heroic Age on Ross Island. Near McMurdo Station was Discovery Hut, built by Scott's team on his first expedition to Antarctica in 1901–04. At Cape Royds, 45 kilometres north of Scott Base, was the hut built by Ernest Shackleton on his 1907–09 expedition. In between these two, at Cape Evans, was the largest of the huts, used by Scott and his expedition during 1910–13. A fourth hut, the first building ever constructed on this continent, was on the mainland at Cape Adare, but our itinerary did not include this remote spot. It was the Ross Island buildings that we would see.

The small print pointed out that dates were flexible in the Antarctic, depending on the weather conditions and transport, and after spending Wednesday around Scott Base we were beginning to worry if our planned travel would ever happen. Sightseeing around the base was, finally, beginning to pall. There was only so much machinery I could take in. But finding out just when we were going anywhere seemed virtually impossible. Natalie seemed evasive, and it felt as if precious time was slipping away.

It was a relief, therefore, when, late on Thursday, Natalie nonchalantly introduced us to one of the Scott Base staff, Keith, who had the strange nickname Spang. He would drive us up the sea ice road the next day. The elliptical way in which we found out about things was frustrating, but it was, I'm sure, in part because no one wanted to get our hopes up when the vagaries of the weather could easily have prevented us from even walking outside. We were grateful to be going. Vikki, Tania, Chris and I would be joined by Lucrezia, who had slowly emerged from her travel sickness. Also joining us would be

Michelle, the executive assistant, and Jane, who had Fridays off from her job looking after the base shop.

We had already had a brief taste of what was to come when we visited the first hut built on Ross Island. Located on its own little point, Hut Point, Discovery Hut was the sentinel of the Heroic Age. It was named after the ship on which Scott sailed down to the southern continent. As we drove in from the sea ice runway, McMurdo Station was on one side of Winter Quarters Bay and the hut on the other. In summer near where *Discovery* was moored US icebreakers pull into the bay, bringing supplies. Each year, over winter, a pier is built by pouring water into the required shape and leaving it to freeze solid. Discovery Hut also bears witness to one of the less savoury aspects of the more recent past. Under the sea ice is the most contaminated water in the Ross Sea region, the legacy of an old rubbish dump and of the previous practice of piling garbage onto the sea ice and leaving it to fall into the water as the ice thawed each year.

In the crisp air, we wandered down a gravel-coated road to the little hut. Tourist groups wanting to visit the Ross Dependency have to check in with New Zealand's Ministry of Foreign Affairs. Foreign tourism operators can baulk at filling out the forms designed to help measure the environmental impact of tourist visits to the historic huts, but they are usually won round when reminded that New Zealand, as caretaker, has the hut keys. Antarctica New Zealand had already filled in all the environmental forms for us, but Natalie gently prised out of us the $20 donation each visitor is asked to make. In return we received a small booklet on the historic huts and a tax receipt. It was, after all, a charitable donation, but keeping this small slip of paper for a New Zealand tax return seemed incongruous somehow.

I already knew the history of the huts but I reread the little booklet. Holding it attested that I really was one of only 3000 or so people who get to see inside these huts each year. Only about 500 of those are tourists — the lucky ones who sail into the Ross Sea region. The majority of Antarctic tourists visit the Antarctic Peninsula, a crooked finger of land the other side of the continent that stretches up toward South America. Tourist boats leave from Ushuaia in Argentina.

From a distance, the Discovery Hut was an unprepossessing squat brown square, almost camouflaged against the piebald hills. But for Natalie this was the most important hut. 'It's the most historically exciting hut. That's because it was used by multiple expeditions over a period of years. And it's amazing to think that all those extraordinary people have stood in that hut,' she explained as we wandered down the hill. From the outside, the hut appeared entirely the wrong shape: its veranda was reminiscent of the bull-nose verandas designed to deflect the searing sun in the outback of Australia. It turned out that the prefabricated hut had indeed been made across the Tasman.

Erecting the building had been no easy matter. The soil, the explorers discovered, was frozen solid just centimetres below the surface; to erect the hut they needed holes about a metre deep. 'Many an hour,' Scott wrote, 'was spent with pick, shovel and crowbar before the solid supports were erected.' Despite this effort, the hut was never meant for permanent habitation: on that journey the expedition slept in the relative comfort of the ship, *Discovery*.

It was from here, in November 1902, that Scott, Ernest Shackleton and Edward Wilson made the first inroads into the continent, trekking as far south as 82°16′ South. Even then, they were still only on the Ross Ice Shelf. They all became ill with scurvy, but Shackleton, the man with the biggest build, became the most ill, having to ride on the sledge at one point of the return journey. Once the trio had returned, and a relief ship came down to the ice, Shackleton was invalided home by Scott. That was, apparently, the start of an intense rivalry between the pair. Just four years after his ignominious departure from Antarctica, Shackleton would leave England, in his ship the *Nimrod*, for his own attempt on the Pole. Later he would attempt the first crossing of the entire continent of the Antarctic. He was successful in neither quest, but was considered a hero for his leadership of his men.

The rivalry between him and Scott is carried on by Antarctic devotees to this day, but Gerald Doorly, an officer on one of the ships that came to the *Discovery*'s relief, wrote in his memoir, *The Voyages of the 'Morning'*, that Scott and Shackleton remained friendly, at least while they were still recovering down south from their ordeal. After they had returned to the comfort of the ship, Doorly wrote, Scott would steal into Wilson's and Shackleton's cabins with fresh supplies from the pantry for the malnourished men. 'I say, Shackles, how would you fancy some sardines on toast?' Doorly heard Scott ask.

A decade later, while the remnants of Scott's last expedition were out looking for the bodies of their leader and his party, the Northern Party, a group of men selected by Scott to carry out scientific work on the coast across from Ross Island, staggered into Discovery Hut. They had been marooned throughout the winter of 1912 on the coast of Victoria Land, when the expedition's ship, the *Terra Nova*, couldn't get through the ice to reach them. Their tents were no match for the constant winds. In order to have a chance of surviving the winter, the men dug an underground cave in the ice. Naval discipline was maintained; men slept on one side, officers the other. They scavenged seals and seaweed to eke out what rations they had left, and they named their miserable home Inexpressible Island. The six men not only survived, but in the spring trudged for 40 days to safety. First stop was the empty Hut Point hut, where they grabbed meagre supplies: rock cakes, butter, onions and some tobacco. Revitalised, they headed north to be reunited with the remaining expedition members at Cape Evans and to learn the news that Scott's polar party were all dead.

For another marooned group, Scott's small first hut was crucial. From 1914–17, it provided shelter for the Ross Sea party, who came to the Antarctic to lay depots of food and fuel supplies for Shackleton's Antarctic crossing attempt. (The crossing never happened: on the other side of the continent, Shackleton's ship *Endurance* was crushed in sea ice, leaving Shackleton with an epic struggle to keep his crew safe.) Laying supply depots was also the role that fell to Sir Edmund Hillary's team 40 years later in the Transantarctic Expedition, led by Briton Dr Vivian Fuchs, which would make the first successful traverse of the continent.

Shackleton's Ross Sea team sailed into Cape Evans on board their ship *Aurora*, which was to be their accommodation. But in May of 1915 an Antarctic storm blew the *Aurora* away from its mooring at Cape Evans. The 10 members of the Ross Sea party who were ashore at the time were stranded. Four were at Cape Evans and six were away on a sledging expedition. Since they had intended to live mainly on the *Aurora*, they had not unloaded food. They had only the clothing they were wearing and little in the way of medical supplies. They had to scavenge what they could from the supplies left in the huts at Cape Evans, Cape Royds and Hut Point. Old tents used by Scott were cut up and made into clothing; for their pipes, they had a carefully blended mix of tea, coffee and sawdust, which they named Hut Point Mixture. Despite being invaded by the ice, the Discovery Hut provided much-needed shelter for the sledging party that first winter. However, they didn't find the stores encased in ice just metres away from the hungry men.

The following year, the team decided that they had to fulfill the task given to them by the Boss, the name given to Shackleton by the men. A team of six managed, with their scavenged supplies, to lay every depot they had been charged with. In doing so, this marooned party spent the most days out sledging on the ice of any of the Heroic Age explorers. Their efforts were the only successful aspect of Shackleton's Imperial Transantarctic Expedition. On returning from this epic journey, during which one of their number died, the team again took shelter at Discovery Hut. They had been prevented from returning to the greater comfort of the Cape Evans hut by dangerously weak sea ice. Eventually two of the party decided to try to walk back to Cape Evans. They died in the attempt.

Shackleton, who had managed to save all his crew on the *Endurance*, did eventually arrive to pick up the surviving Ross Sea men, but from the wrong direction. The *Aurora* had, amazingly, made it back to New Zealand after drifting north for almost a year. So it was from the bow of the *Aurora* that Shackleton finally hailed his men. When Shackleton's men finally closed the doors of the Ross Island huts, it was the end of the Heroic Age.

In the early 1960s the encroaching ice was dug out of the old wooden buildings on Ross Island and visitors started filing through. In the ensuing years, conservation was well-meaning, but piecemeal; perhaps the odd window fixed here or there, roofs repaired and relics rearranged. Many had assumed that the cold, dry climate would preserve the huts, but after nearly a hundred years of exposure to the harsh Antarctic climate, they are clearly starting to fall apart.

It is the salt in the sea water that is breaking down the wood in the three huts, according to scientists from the universities of Waikato and Minnesota. In the Antarctic summer, snow and ground ice melt, providing moisture that dissolves salts from soils and from the sea, which are then dispersed by Antarctica's fierce winds. The constant grinding by the salt detaches and erodes the wood fibres, giving it a furry appearance — it looks as if someone has scrubbed it with a pot scourer. The process is relatively slow, but over many years very severe damage can occur. The deterioration has probably accelerated in the last 40 years because the huts are now so exposed, Roberta Farrell, an effervescent professor from the University of Waikato, told me before I left for the ice. 'They were totally snowbanked and encased in ice [before the 1960s] and that probably helped hold them better, although nobody could see them.' One of her specialities was studying the wood the huts were made of. I spotted a mosaic of small tiles of wood tacked to a huge billboard on the hill above Shackleton's hut at Cape Royds. It had to be one of her wood-testing experiments.

Understanding just what the huts are made of is crucial to any future conservation efforts, but it hasn't always been easy. Some of the timber for the Discovery Hut came from London, but the records of the timber agents have been destroyed, probably in World War II bombing. So, when a piece of Discovery Hut timber, removed in the 1960s, was handed on to Farrell she found out that the wood, which had been thought to be Douglas fir, was actually Pinus sylvestris.

Roberta Farrell's painstaking work is one of the strands that the Antarctic Heritage Trust is drawing together in its ambitious campaign to save the huts. In the last few years, the trust, formed in 1987, has decided to change its approach and develop professional conservation plans for each of the hut sites. 'We've basically put up our hands and said, this stuff is going down the gurgler unless we do something,' the trust's energetic chief executive Nigel Watson told me. Visitors' $20 donations clearly won't be enough.

Later that summer the trust took the Princess Royal down to the ice to commemorate the centenary of Scott's visit.

Princess Anne handed over £70,000 from the British Antarctic Territory. The territory, which has its own government somewhere in Whitehall (another of those mind-bending Antarctic legal twists), earns income from stamps and the tax paid by its resident scientists. Apparently, if they are there long enough to satisfy residency requirements, they can elect to be taxed there, rather than the UK. The New Zealand government has contributed $350,000 to the trust and the philanthropic Getty Grant programme — part of the J. Paul Getty Trust based in Los Angeles — has added $200,000. In total, the trust wants to raise $NZ30 million for the restoration of the three Ross Island huts and the one on the continent at Cape Adare.

Tourist numbers — either private or, like me, supported by national programmes — are on the rise. Most of them make the journey to the more accessible Antarctic Peninsula, but, with the lure of those modest but historic huts, the Ross Sea region will be increasingly attractive. To many the idea of increasing tourism is anathema, but others believe it is inevitable. Commercial flights to the ice and accommodation on this side of Antarctica might even be part of the continent's future. But would the huts withstand the onslaught of planeloads of tourists? The trust aims to make it so; gone are the days when visitors could just pilfer a small souvenir. Nowadays there are strict rules to follow on entering the huts: we had to scrape the snow off the bottom of our boots with brushes, we were exhorted not to touch anything and only a few of us could enter at a time.

Near Discovery Hut stands a memorial to George Vince, a seaman who slid to his death — down a cliff and into the water below — during the first Scott expedition. His body was never found. It was the second death on that voyage: Charles Bonner fell to his death after climbing up a mast to wave to the cheering Lyttelton crowds. Chris and I wandered over to Vince's cross to await our turn to enter the Discovery Hut; his fate haunted me every time my boots wobbled on the ice.

Outside the hut, we paused to look at a plaque proclaiming its historic monument status. Inside the cluttered mélange of polar exploration debris pointed to the hut's importance, not just for Scott, but for all the explorers in the early years of the 20th century. Boxes from the first Scott expedition, the British Antarctic Expedition shore party, mingled with boxes from later journeys: Colman's mustard, Fry's Pure Cocoa, Cerebos salt and Bovril sledging rations were jumbled together in a mess on the floor. This was, of course, part of the corporate support these old expeditions had to secure. It was as essential then as it has been for later expeditions, but it is a task few enjoy. Sir Edmund Hillary once described fundraising with typical understatement as 'a somewhat distasteful business'. However, for me the familiar brands were a comforting link between my pantry and those early adventurers. On one shelf stood a rusty primus, identical to the one I had struggled with on survival training. A pair of trousers was draped over a makeshift clothes-line. Near the door hung the carcass of a sheep, one of 45 that New Zealand donated to the expedition, and the mummified remains of a half-plundered seal. Blubber from seals was the main heating fuel for the huts and the interior was a grimy black as a result. The fascination of this venerated hut, as Natalie pointed out, was actually the rubbish the explorers had left behind. She took a photo of the dainty ice crystals coating the inside of the roof. I followed suit — the gleaming white against the brown was the prettiest aspect of the gloomy hut. Natalie was looking for patterns, she said, to use in her Antarctic quilts. A makeshift stove — just a sheet of iron over an open fire — held a frying pan filled with blackened scraps of seal meat, giving an eerie impression that the last occupants had just stood up and left abruptly. It was, I realised, only a simulacrum of how the explorers had lived, but enough remained to evoke the reality of their courageous journeys.

I had already been to pay homage to the Antarctic adventurers back in New Zealand. Buried in Wellington's sprawling Karori cemetery were two survivors of Shackleton's *Endurance* voyage, Thomas Orde Lees and Harry McNeish. McNeish, the ship's carpenter, had come to New Zealand after *Endurance*, unable to settle to life in England. He lived and died in poverty on Wellington's docks, according to Carolyn Alexander's book *The Endurance*, but a Royal Navy ship provided pallbearers for his coffin and the New Zealand Army supplied a gun carriage to carry it. His grave at Karori cemetery was unmarked until 1957, when the New Zealand Antarctic Society erected a headstone. Shackleton had refused to award McNeish the Polar Medal, a sad end for the carpenter whose skills maintained the boat in which Shackleton's crew made their epic 1300-kilometre journey to South Georgia. He was also the man who patiently screwed nails into the boots of Shackleton, Crean and Worsley before their traverse of South Georgia to safety and rescue. I pulled the onion grass out of the cracks on McNeish's grave before I left — a tiny tribute to a man of strength and determination.

It was Orde Lees who fascinated me most, however. He joined Shackleton's Imperial Transantarctic Expedition in 1914 — a superbly fit captain in the Royal Marines. Orde Lees loathed being in a small ship. 'I expect to expire about the 12th,' he wrote in his journal. 'Eat nothing. Sea sick and homesick all day.' He also hated having to work alongside merchant navy crew and, worst of all, having to scrub spit off the decks. The habit of expectoration, he wrote, 'would not be tolerated for a moment in a man o' war'. He wasn't always priggish: he relished the chance to show off his physical prowess, shimmying up the mast to help furl the topsail. 'I don't want to boast, but I am the only one besides the sailors that cares to go aloft at all.'

Orde Lees was the ski expert and motor mechanic of the expedition, but neither skill was needed after the expedition's ship, the *Endurance*, was crushed in pack ice. So Shackleton, now lauded for his management of his men, found an outlet for Orde Lees's energy and fussy attention to detail in the storage and disbursement of the ship's stores. 'The importance of perfect packing cannot be too energetically insisted upon,' Orde Lees wrote in a letter home. After the rescue in 1916, Orde Lees entered the Royal Flying Corps and there funnelled his energies — and his aptitude for heights — into persuading the authorities that pilots should be allowed to use parachutes.

He once demonstrated the efficacy of the parachute by leaping off the Tower Bridge into the Thames, a mere 45 metres below. After World War I, he continued to demonstrate the parachute in many places — he was the 'daring British aviator' who leapt out of a plane near the Statue of Liberty in 1919. In that same year, in a stunt for the *Daily Mail*, he parachuted onto an Aberdeen golf course carrying a small suitcase in one hand and an umbrella in the other.

Parachuting took Orde Lees to Japan in 1921, where he taught the skill to the Japanese military and laid claim to being the first to make a winter climb of Fujiyama. He also lectured at Kobe University, read the English news over the radio, and was for three years correspondent for the *Times*. He married there for the second time but, with Japan's entry into the war looking imminent, Orde Lees wrenched himself, his wife and his daughter away from their comfortable Tokyo life and sailed to Wellington. They left virtually all their possessions behind. By now 61, he was forced to accept whatever work was available and he became the office lackey at the New Zealand Correspondence School. It was, a friend recalled, 'the least pleasant of his adventures'. He still spiced his life with a dash of the unusual, however: in a conformist age, he wore sandshoes and jogged around Wellington and once rode a bicycle down Parliament's steps.

When the Byrd Antarctic expedition came to Wellington, 70-year-old Orde Lees went for a flight in one of the expedition's helicopters. He also attended some of the very first planning meetings for the 1957 expedition that would see a New Zealand team supporting the first crossing of

Antarctica. The help he could give must have been limited: Shackleton's team hadn't even reached the continent, and Orde Lees was by then an old man.

By all accounts, Orde Lees's personality failed to charm his companions as much as his exploits charmed me. On *Endurance* he was apparently the least liked member of the team. He snored, he hoarded food, and on the sea journey to their Elephant Island refuge he proved so ineffectual at rowing that he was relegated to the bottom of the boat, where he slept as the others rowed for their lives. He also irritated to the end, it seems. At the Correspondence School, 'he used to make much of his Antarctic experiences and was apparently an arrogant "Pom" with a great opinion of his own importance' an old acquaintance wrote to me. Not everyone in dull, unimaginative 1950s New Zealand was so harsh with the old adventurer. After cleaning Orde Lees's medals a few years after his death in 1958, Captain Geoffrey Stagg wrote: 'I bet if he were alive today he would be pressing a claim to be the first man to be rocketed to the moon.'

In fact, these men could have been going to the moon: they stayed out of touch far longer than any modern-day astronaut. It was almost a year before anyone beyond Cape Evans knew of the death of Scott and his companions in 1912. I heard the first words of the first man to set foot on the moon from a crackly classroom speaker in the small country town of Tuakau in July 1969. Just quite who was the first to set foot on the southern continent will probably never be known. But I like to think it was a New Zealander. Just over 100 years ago, 17-year-old Alexander von Tunzelman from Stewart

Island signed on to an Antarctic expedition led by Henryk Bull. On 24 January 1895, the expedition made what it claimed was the first landing on the mainland of Antarctica. Others on von Tunzelman's ship claimed the glory of that first step, but, to his dying day, von Tunzelman insisted that he was the first ashore. He had had to jump out to steady the boat for the leaders of the expedition.

Discovery Hut had given us an idea of what to expect, but we were all excited when, on Friday morning, we started to pack up the Hägglunds. This tracked vehicle would be our transport on our journey to the huts at Cape Evans and Cape Royds. We had made our own lunch: sandwiches, drinks and muesli bars. We hoped this time that the polystyrene bins would keep the sandwiches from freezing. Lashed to the roof of the Hägglunds were the survival packs we had learned about in training. The most disconcerting aspect of our briefing from Spang, the driver, was the instruction for exiting the amphibious craft, should it break through the sea ice into the water below. There was a window in the ceiling of the front section out of which we were supposed to scramble. In the rear section of the vehicle — a tractor cabin that was hooked on like a trailer — the idea was to shimmy out the windows on the sides, which apparently popped out. In the gorgeous sunshine with a china-plate-white road stretching ahead of us, it seemed inconceivable that anything could go wrong. Nonetheless, we all paid close attention to Spang's words of caution.

The back tractor cabin had no view — the windows quickly

iced over — so we took turns riding there. For some, the gentle rocking of the Hägglunds, once we got going, was a welcome soporific. Thursday night had been the DVs' last night on base and American night at the bar; it had been a big night for some. Lucrezia was exhausted for a different reason: having been late once before, she had been warned not to be tardy for that morning's departure. Her room-mates had seen her donning all her extreme-cold-weather gear at the impossibly early time of 2 a.m. Someone finally convinced her it was too early to be awake and it turned out that it wasn't just her jet-lagged head that was topsy-turvy. Her watch had been on upside down.

The journey to Cape Evans took an hour and a half in a Hägglunds, which trundles along at about 15 kilometres an hour. Probably to relieve the lack of driving challenge, our driver seemed to take delight in almost — but not quite — shaving the flags off the bamboo poles that marked the sea ice route. The road wended its way up the coast of Ross Island; here and there, small smudges that were the encampments of scientists peppered the sea ice. When we pulled up at Cape Evans, there were two science camps nearby, one US and one Kiwi. We disembarked to walk across the sea ice to the hut. Directly behind it, faint curves of cloud floated on either side of Erebus, bracketing its grandeur. The sea ice was slowly loosening its winter grip at the shore, and tide cracks were beginning to appear. We had been told, rather improbably, that flinging your arms out as you slid into the sea would stop you from sinking in. Lucrezia walked, apparently oblivious, towards a tide crack that I was negotiating gingerly. 'Watch out!' we all yelled, with an urgency that would have communicated over any language barrier.

The hut at Cape Evans was Scott's second Antarctic hut (after Discovery), used during the 1910–13 expedition. It had no veranda: instead there was a sloping roof and straight walls. Leaning against the outside of the hut were the remains of some of the sledges the expedition had used. Inside the entranceway, a pile of seal blubber was still oozing. In the stables, straw for the expedition's ponies was piled on the ground (like Shackleton's motor car, the ponies were not a great success on the ice). An old hockey stick leant against a wall. Amid the clutter of food stores in the stables, a waxed ball of Dutch cheese lay beside a still-intact water biscuit.

The hut's dim light and coating of blubbery smoke, and our knowledge of the explorers' fate, made it a powerfully gloomy place. But, compared to the dingy Discovery Hut, this was a palace. You could still imagine the excitement and optimism those living here must have once felt. Down the centre of the hut was a dining table, strewn with bottles of chemicals and instruments, remnants of the scientific experiments they had done there. It was at this table that the men had gathered for Scott's 43rd birthday on 6 June 1911, famously captured on film by Herbert Ponting, the expedition's photographer. They held their evening lectures here, too, giving their winter evenings a structure that echoes even now in Antarctic life. It was from this hut that the first Antarctic telephone link was established in September 1911. A thin aluminium wire telephone line was rigged up one spring from Cape Evans to Hut Point, but it was never expected to withstand the winter blizzards and lasted for that one spring only. These days the phone number for 'Scott Base, Antarctica' is nestled discreetly below the listing for Antarctica New Zealand in the Christchurch phone book.

In the kitchen, canned clutter abounded. Even after years of casual pilfering, this biggest of all the huts is still packed with more than 10,000 items. The bright yellow of the boxes of Fry's Pure Cocoa provided a splash of colour amid the prevailing rust. Once again, the condiments — Cerebos salt and Colman's mustard — reached across the centuries. It had all, no doubt, been rearranged over the years according to the varying notions of eager conservationists, but we still looked on those cans with quiet awe.

At the other end of the hut, tucked around a corner, was Scott's bed, sporting a reindeer sleeping bag. The gloom was lifted here by a small window filled with blue Antarctic sky. Under the window was a chart table; it was in this nook that Scott wrote his journals. Natalie told us that the table wasn't original, and the stuffed penguin laid across the table had been left by Shackleton's Ross Sea party. But, even though the nook had been stripped virtually bare over the years, I felt as if I were intruding in a private space. Scott's friend Bill Wilson and his second-in-command Teddy Evans had slept opposite him. It wasn't hard to imagine the trio chatting far into the night in this private corner. The feeling of trespass was even more intense in the cramped darkroom used by Herbert Ponting, the 'camera artist', as he preferred to be called. This pokey room was cluttered with chemicals and an occasional glass plate. Nails poking out of wooden boards had held in place the first movie to be shot here, so that it could be developed. I desperately wanted to pick up one of the glass plates to peer into the past, but felt honour-bound to respect the rules. My eyes, not my fingers, caressed the glass plates.

Further down the hut were the so-called 'tenements'. Here slept Henry Bowers, nicknamed Birdie because of his large nose. Short, but incredibly strong, he was a late addition to the team and had to walk to the Pole because no skis had been packed for a fifth man. He made it almost all the way back, but died with Scott in the tent just 20 kilometres from a food depot that might have saved their lives. On the bunk next to him slept Lawrence 'Titus' Oates, one of the world's most celebrated suicides. Still pinned above the bed were a couple of pieces of cardboard, onto which were stuck small pictures of dogs, cut from magazines. The young Aspley Cherry-Garrard, whose book *The Worst Journey in the World* is considered by many to be one of the best ever written about Antarctic adventures, and adventures in general, had been tucked under Bowers on the bottom bunk. Old snowshoes for the mules, sent out in the second year as a gift from the Indian government, hung over the end of the bed. (The mules were used in the search for Scott, but all were shot before the surviving members of the party returned to New Zealand.) Clothing and shoes littered other beds. A wall of boxes had helped to keep a semblance of naval rigour intact, separating officers from the men. It remains partially intact. Above the bed of Birdie Bowers, tucked into one of the ubiquitous Colman's boxes, was a battered felt hat.

In reality this hut, like the one down the coast, was a sad, decaying museum. Though the whole place was resonant with the explorers' presence, I didn't expect to hear the door rattling as a sledging party returned. Still, I didn't want to consign the memory of these men to the past. Their achievements were too big. Back at Discovery Hut I had written the words 'Just for one day', sure that those following me would read this and hear the haunting chorus of the David Bowie song 'Heroes'. But here that seemed a little too flippant: 'Heroes for every age', I finally wrote in the visitors' book at Scott's hut.

Jane was hovering as I flicked back through the pages of the visitors' book, curious to see what others had written. 'Can I have a look now?' she asked politely, but insistently. My time was up, so I handed over the book and meandered out of the hut and into what had been the stables. I poked my head into each stall, hoping to find the pony feed that was supposedly still intact. I slipped off my glove to take a photo and then, to my horror, I couldn't find it again. It was absolutely forbidden to leave the smallest thing behind, anywhere in the Antarctic, much less a glove in the stables of Scott's sanctum. I was peering anxiously into the debris, already rehearsing my confession to Natalie, when the glove fell to the floor. It had been caught in my many layers of clothing.

Relieved, I went outside, stopping to look at those parts of the *Aurora*'s anchor not covered in snow. The anchor was mute testament to the blizzards we never encountered on our trip; it had stayed stuck fast while the ship it was supposed to moor had been blown away. Behind the hut, Chris and I climbed up a hill, past the meteorological instruments from which Scott's team gathered weather data. Their methodical efforts live on in the annals of meteorology, and the data is still useful to modern-day scientists as they try to unravel the past and predict the future of Earth's climate.

Also on Weathervane Hill was another simple cross, a memorial to the three men who died in Shackleton's Ross Sea party. From the hilltop we could see the Barne Glacier to the north. Beyond that was our next stop, Shackleton's hut. I could see the rest of our team heading back to the Hägglunds and we went back down the hill to join them. As I walked, a man wandered up to me and asked if he could have a look inside the hut. He was a Kiwi, he explained, working at a US science camp. Such a casual request seemed to be at odds with the detailed environmental impact reports filed on our behalf and the careful briefings we had had. But I guess he figured that this might be his only chance. So I pointed out our driver, who was just locking up. I'm not sure whether he managed to make it into the hut but I hope so.

We distributed ourselves around the Hägglunds and set off for Cape Royds, driving past the Barne Glacier and over the Barne crack, a tiny sliver of water visible only in summer — the first sign of the sea ice melting. Britain's Princess Anne, making the same pilgrimage later in that season, had to fly by helicopter to Cape Royds: the sea ice was no longer safe. We chugged the 11 kilometres further north along the coast to Royds and found some Americans arriving on skidoos — motorised toboggans for the ice — at the same time. They were having some brief recreation before heading out on a long expedition to a remote destination on the continent, and we decided to have our lunch and toilet stop first, allowing the group from McMurdo the first look around.

We chewed quickly through the muesli bars and sandwiches with their various fillings concocted by Tania and Vikki. As instructed, we were drinking water pretty much constantly. Lunch was eaten standing up and walking around; though it was a sunny day, it is never a good idea to stand stock-still in the Antarctic, as the chill air soon worms its way in. By now, however, there was no way I could ignore the querulous demands of my bladder. I retrieved my Freshette from a pocket and wandered toward the 'pee pole' some distance away. Tania offered to take an action shot, but I was feeling a lot less confident than I had been back in the base toilet. We hadn't been wearing our ECWs then. The zip on the salopettes goes from the top of the bib to the bottom of the torso, and can be unzipped from either end. Inserting my Freshette was supposed to be a simple matter of unzipping at the bottom, but my outer swathing of jackets meant that I just couldn't reach down and find the small tag at the end of the zipper. Momentarily defeated, I hurried back to the group to ask an amused Natalie to unzip me. Then it was back, as briskly as possible in my mukluks, to the 'pee pole'. I squeezed the Freshette cup into the opening, extended the tube and aimed, I hoped, at the yellow snow near the pole.

Much relieved, I wandered back to join the rest of the group. By now they were sitting on the American skidoos. Our programme didn't call for a ride on the New Zealand ones back at the base, so this was Tania and Vikki's skidoo photo opportunity. They flung their heads and bodies back and clung on tight, feigning movement as Chris took a quick photo and Natalie smiled benignly on her naughty charges.

The Americans returned and we waved them off, then it was our turn to head over a small hill to the spot Shackleton's team had chosen for their home from 1908 until 1909. Originally Shackleton had wanted to set up his base at Hut Point, making use of the only building then on Ross Island, the Discovery Hut. However, after their falling-out, Scott had forbidden Shackleton from using the Discovery area and Shackleton had to think again. He decided to set up camp on the Great Ice Barrier, as the Ross Ice Shelf was then known, but when he arrived in the *Nimrod* in 1908 he realised that it was too dangerous. The shape of the ice shelf had changed dramatically since Shackleton had last seen it in 1902, indicating that huge icebergs had fallen from its edges. For safety, he decided that they would have to establish their base on land, not ice, and so Shackleton returned to Ross Island. He chose Cape Royds, and the better deal as far as Ross Island locales went I decided. The hut had a view of the mountains and the most southerly colony of Adélie penguins in the world was on its doorstep. In warmer weather, the men would have had the beach almost at their front door.

Tania, Vikki and I climbed to the top of a crag overlooking the Adélie penguin colony. At this time of year, Adélie penguins came ashore to mate. It was early in the season, however, and the penguins were still sparse. Nor was this to be a good year for them. By the end of that season, the scientists who study penguins estimated that this Adélie colony had only managed to produce about one percent of their usual tally of chicks.

The culprits were the descendants of the iceberg that first lured me to the Antarctic. That massive berg had broken into two pieces, which had floated into position between Beaufort Island and Franklin Island north of Ross Island. The talk was that this was why the sea ice in McMurdo Sound had refused to break up. For the penguins it was a formidable obstacle between them and the sea — their source of food. Waddling along at only two kilometres an hour, the penguins had to travel up to 50 kilometres further than usual. Either they died, or their chick died before they could return, or they just became completely befuddled. Later in the season a penguin wandered so far south that it ended up dying on the sea ice runway.

Even so, on the afternoon we visited, the birds congregating to build nests were making a businesslike racket. The strange noise sounded just like rattles being twirled around the heads of excited football fans. I sat entranced, listening to the harsh cadence of their calls and watching as they sunned themselves, fought or just waddled. They were the first living creatures, other than a lone skua, the scavenging Antarctic bird, that I had seen in Antarctica. I was, like so many others, charmed by their short black and white bodies, flapping wings and scurrying walk. The penguins were weaving in and out of a sort of penguin corral. Scientists studying the Adélies put this fence up each season. To get in and out, the penguins have to pass through stiles, where they are unobtrusively weighed.

Down below, we could see the others coming out of the hut, so we left our vantage point to go down. We were supposed to take a curved route back to the hut, in order to stay clear of a protected area. Despite my best efforts to stay behind the imagined lines, I somehow strayed, and had to be yelled at by the ever vigilant Natalie.

Entering Shackleton's hut soon dispelled any feelings of indignity. The sunlight streamed into this hut, giving it a companionable air. Shackleton seemed to have run a more egalitarian hut than Scott. A small room to the right of the door served as Shackleton's sleeping quarters and office; everyone else slept in the main hut. A large coal range at the end of the hut would once have exuded welcome warmth and a lighting system still rigged above the main door provided illumination. Hanging on one wall was a photo of King Edward VII of England and Queen Alexandra. The royal couple had visited the *Nimrod* before it sailed, giving Shackleton a Union Jack to hoist on the ice. On a shelf, dry and dusty pages of a book sat open at a chapter entitled 'The Woman and the Poet'. Bags of flake tapioca and calavances — a beady starch and beans familiar in my grandfather's time, but little seen today — were tidily packed against a wall. The familiar Colman's boxes and tins of Huntley and Palmers 'Superior Reading Biscuits' were scattered around the kitchen area. In this hut, space was more constrained; to make room, the dining table was hoisted into the ceiling after meals. Tucked under a bench were a row of boots. We had been told to look for the dog kennels around the side of the hut, but they and the mummified remains of a dog still lay buried under the ice. It was the closest we would get to a domestic animal in Antarctica. By 1994 all the huskies had been evicted for environmental reasons.

It was from this hut that Shackleton led his expedition to

the Pole. It was an undertaking that inspired thousands: when Shackleton's ship *Nimrod* sailed south, it is estimated that 30,000 people farewelled it from Lyttelton. Shackleton went as far south as anyone had gone at that time — 88°23′ south — but he turned back 120 kilometres short of the South Pole to save the lives of his men. 'Better a live donkey than a dead lion,' he famously told his wife, though he was bitterly disappointed not to reach his goal. There were many other firsts for the expedition, however. Men from Shackleton's team — including geologist Edgeworth David, physicist Douglas Mawson and surgeon Alistair Mackay — made the first ascent of Erebus. Its lower slopes were tantalisingly close to the Cape Royds hut. That same trio were first to claim the geological prize of reaching the South Magnetic Pole in 1909.

It was in this hut that the continent's first book was printed. Shackleton's expedition had planned the enterprise to keep the tedium of winter at bay. They had brought a printing press, an etching press and large quantities of paper and ink for the purpose, all transported on the *Nimrod*. In the winter of 1908 various expedition members produced about a hundred copies of the 120-page illustrated book. They used board from the packing cases as covers; the printed pages were sewn together and the spine was bound with sealskin. Shackleton edited the book, which was entitled *Aurora Australis*, after Antarctica's spectacular winter light show, the Southern Lights.

The hut was also the scene of another Antarctic first. In a garage once appended to the outside of the hut, and long since collapsed, the continent's first car was housed, an Arrol-Johnston. It was donated to the expedition by Shackleton's patron Sir William Beardmore, but was next to useless on the ice. Tracked, not wheeled, vehicles would dominate here.

Our brief foray into the past was coming to an end. It was time to head back to Scott Base and dinner. Spang locked up the hut and we headed up over the hill to the Hägglunds. Having slaked our thirst for history, we took in some of the tourist sights. Spang stopped the Hägglunds by the Barne Glacier and we all took turns being photographed standing beside it, dwarfed by the stream of ice that sloughed off the slopes of Mt Erebus. By now, I was so accustomed to the white around me that it no longer seemed just white; it was clearly in varying shades. The ice in the cliffs was a dense blue white, the pitted sea ice was grey white and over the top of the edge of the glacier the streaky black and white of the top of Erebus was just visible. The sky was a saturated blue.

Further down the sea route we trundled to a halt once more. About 10 Weddell seals, the southernmost naturally occurring mammals on earth, were on the ice. It was important, Natalie warned us, not to get between the seals and their hole. Not much chance of that, I thought, remembering how quickly death could come to anyone who fell through a hole. I stood as close as I could to photograph one plump specimen. The seal lifted up its head to look me over, and then went back to sleep. Its round brown eyes, slightly upturned mouth and frisky whiskers gave it an appealing look. Some of the other seals were less attractive, with gashes on their coats and blood smeared around them on the ice. The gashes could have been the result of killer whales or leopard seals attacking them, or simply male rivalry.

The seals were, it has to be said, as inelegant as slugs atop the ice. Below the ice was another matter. At the science lecture at McMurdo we would see their pelagic ballet, captured by cameras strapped onto their backs. Sadly, we were too early in the season for pups. I had hoped to see a baby seal. In the first six weeks of their life they quadruple their birth weight, inflating like little Yorkshire puddings.

Our final stop was to be the ice caves, fabled among Scott Base visitors. They are little notches at the end of the Erebus Ice Tongue, another great slab of ice that sprawls out into the sea from the island's volcano. We were planning to slip into the two caves at the tip of the tongue. Once more we tumbled out of the Hägglunds and crossed slippery ice to reach the entrances. To get into the first small cave we had to slide on our stomachs down a narrow chute. I was reluctant at first, but Spang threatened to push me down the entrance if I didn't slide in, so I propelled myself forward. I regretted it immediately. It felt as if I was clinging to the side of an icy white drainpipe and that at any moment I would slide into the void. Jane and Natalie were already inside in an icy nook, leaning back against the wall. I ended up slightly lower down, pressing my body into the side of the wall, my mukluks making a very small indentation in the ice. I was reassured by Natalie that dropping to the floor of the cave just a metre or so below was the worst that could possibly happen, but not even the translucent beauty of the ice could prevent my feelings of rising panic. Ignominiously, I was levered out the way I had come.

Mercifully, the second cave was much bigger, and we could move around, admiring the strange curves and bumps inside

111

the tip of the glacier. It was necessary to move carefully, however, since the floor was polished to a slippery sheen. We took turns leaning against a sheer wall, sinking into the dusting of pastel blue snow. Icicles and twinkling bunches of ice crystals covered the roof of the cave, and as we moved deeper into the glacier, to where the ice was thickest, the light in the cave turned an even deeper blue. With its soaring roof and light streaming through the cracks in the ice, this was Antarctica's version of a cathedral. It was a magical experience until I lost my footing on the ice and fell to the floor. I landed face down, the hard ice grazing my cheek. My tears, more from shock than real pain, turned crinkly in the cold, but the others quickly helped me to my feet. I rode in the front of the Hägglunds on the way back, consoling myself that at least I had the best view.

Apparently everyone who makes the journey to the huts comes away with a favourite, and as we lumbered back over the flag-marked ice route, Natalie asked me which was mine. I found it hard to favour one hut over another. Shackleton's hut was light and airy and felt to me as if it would have been a companionable place; Scott's Discovery Hut held the memories of many and helped start it all; and no one could leave the tenebrous interior of Scott's hut at Cape Evans without thinking of the 20 kilometres that separated the survivors of the Pole journey from their last food depot. As I tried to sift through the competing images, I recalled my first visit to Japan. I had entered the courtyard containing the fabled dry rock garden of the Ryoanji Temple in Kyoto, not really knowing what to expect. Like everyone else filing past the

Discovery Hut, built by Scott on his first trip to the Antarctic, stands guard over Winter Quarters Bay. McMurdo Station is in the background. PHOTO: CHRIS ARCUS

The hut at Cape Evans to which Scott and his four companions never returned.
PHOTO: CHRIS ARCUS

Snow coats the old tools hanging in the porch of Scott's hut at Cape Evans.
PHOTO: CHRIS ARCUS

In the stables of Scott's Cape Evans hut are this very mature ball of cheese and some rather dry biscuits.

In this nook slept Captain Scott. A reindeer-skin sleeping bag remains on the bed.

One hundred years on, the pile of seal blubber continues to ooze.

Of all the early explorers Shackleton, who made his home here at Cape Royds, had the best view. PHOTO: CHRIS ARCUS

On a shelf in Shackleton's hut sit the fragile pages of a book, fallen open at the chapter entitled 'The Woman and The Poet'.

The stocks of food— egg powder, pea soup and flake tapioca — have a decidedly old-fashioned flavour.

The kitchen corner in Shackleton's hut at Cape Royds.

This modest hut at Scott Base, built by the Transantarctic Expedition, is being turned into a museum. A towel still hangs in Sir Edmund Hillary's bedroom. PHOTO: CHRIS ARCUS

Two New Zealand divers prepare to enter the frigid Antarctic waters.

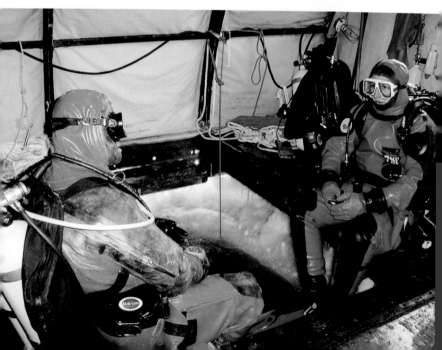

Handling an ice core is not as easy as it might look.

The Wright Valley is part of the biggest ice-free area in Antarctica, the Dry Valleys. It is the closest place on Earth to the landscape of Mars.
PHOTO: CHRIS ARCUS

Tania holds my legs aloft and I finally succeed in my attempt at a headstand on the sea ice.
PHOTO: TANIA McBRIDE/ VIKKI PINK

In the cosy dark of the Starlifter flying northward home, exhaustion overwhelms me. PHOTO: TANIA McBRIDE/VIKKI PINK

carefully placed rocks and finely raked sand, the serenity of the place washed over me. But my favourite memory was of a row of buckets tucked under a nearby bench. They were filled with water, ready to douse any fire in the wooden temple. In the huts, the polar detritus that remained was also carefully placed and raked, but the boots still neatly lined up underneath a bench in Shackleton's hut were all that was really needed to recall the men who had first walked here. The simple wooden huts were indeed monuments to bravery.

That evening at the base I excused myself from my usually frenetic writing schedule. I decided I would need to digest the day's experiences before I could begin to capture them in words. I gave myself the night off and just enjoyed the ambience of the mess and, for a while, the bar. The staff's initial reticence was wearing off and I was also seeing beyond their job titles. Everyone here was passionate about Antarctica. And that, combined with mutual respect for the skills and expertise assembled there, created the social glue. For a few brief days, I had been able to ignore my domestic and familial responsibilities and luxuriate in an Antarctic obsession, happy to find others who would indulge me. This was, clearly, a very seductive world. The rule of thumb, according to McMurdo workers, was that the first year on the ice was for the adventure, the second year for the money, and the third year was because you no longer fitted in anywhere else.

We visited McMurdo the next night to watch *90 Degrees South*, the film made by Scott's photographer, Herbert Ponting. This jaunty little film (some pictures were sped up to keep time with the music) was developed in the darkroom I had seen just a day before. And there, smiling broadly at the camera, was Birdie Bowers, wearing that same battered felt hat.

Later, when I returned to New Zealand, I went to a dinner at a Christchurch hotel in memory of Scott and his officers. They had been entertained there exactly 100 years earlier. The menu was a slimmed-down version of the same extravagant offerings made to the men of the *Discovery*, but the European wines of last century were now proudly Kiwi. The evening's eating was peppered with toasts and speeches; a duo of local identities belted out a rendition of a toast that had been sung to Scott before his first trip to the ice; and home-grown Antarctic explorer Sir Edmund Hillary replaced Scott as the star turn.

Before the dinner started, I had sidled shyly up to Sir Edmund Hillary to show him the 'share certificate' my aunt and uncle bought back in the 1950s to help raise funds for his Transantarctic trip. 'Shall I sign it for you?' he asked genially. I declined, but lingered for a moment, simply enjoying his presence. It must have been the same for the hordes who turned out to see Scott and Shackleton. I told Sir Edmund that my interest in the dinner came from having been to the ice and Lady Hillary, ever mindful of her octogenarian husband's legacy, reminded me that the hut from the Transantarctic Expedition was now just as old as the Heroic Age huts had been when they were uncovered.

Hillary was first asked to join the Transantarctic Expedition in 1953, the same year he conquered Everest with Sherpa Tenzing Norgay. British explorer Dr Vivian Fuchs planned to make the first crossing of Antarctica from the Weddell Sea (the area where pack ice had crushed Shackleton's *Endurance*) to the Ross Sea, via the South Pole. In order to make this epic crossing, Fuchs would need supply depots dotted from the South Pole to the Ross Sea edge of Antarctica. Lanky, laconic Hillary, whose response to reaching the top of the world's highest mountain was, 'We knocked the bastard off', seemed the ideal Antipodean for the job.

The mountaineer, knighted in 1953 by the newly crowned Queen Elizabeth II, set about galvanising the New Zealand government into shouldering its responsibilities in the Ross Dependency. Taking part in both Fuchs's Transantarctic Expedition and the International Geophysical Year (actually 18 months, from 1957 until the end of 1958) would make a reality of New Zealand's Antarctic pretensions. Hillary was duly appointed as leader of the nascent New Zealand Antarctic base. He also became the Ross Dependency's magistrate and postmaster. (He wasn't the first postmaster in the Dependency, however. That honour had been bestowed on Shackleton when he went south in 1908.)

Preparations for the expedition were extensive: Hillary travelled to Norway to test the converted farm tractors he would use in the crossing; he also went to the Weddell Sea to learn more about the conditions. It was there that one of the team's exceptional pilots, John Claydon, tested an amphibian plane known as the *Auster*. To take off, Claydon taxied through a pool in the ice, lifting off with barely enough room to clear the ice wall that ringed the pool. He had decided that there could only be one attempt, Hillary reports in his book *No*

Latitude for Error. He didn't think he'd have the nerve for a second try.

Eventually the expedition was ready and, just before Christmas 1956, the *Endeavour* slipped away from the southern New Zealand town of Bluff. The rugged latitudes — the Roaring Forties segue into the Furious Fifties and then into the Screaming Sixties — buffeted the *Endeavour* and its crew and passengers. A vicious storm on New Year's Day was 'most unpleasant', Hillary wrote dryly. On the other side of the storm was Antarctica. From the ship Hillary could see the mountains Erebus and Terror, but pack ice prevented the ship from approaching until the icebreaker *Glacier* arrived to plough a passage for the New Zealand ship. The Americans continued their hospitable support, encouraging the New Zealanders to settle nearby. And so, on 20 January 1957, Scott Base was opened. The following month *Endeavour* returned to New Zealand.

Before settling the team into their winter home, Hillary wanted to test the expedition tractors on a long trip. It was decided they would travel to a cape on the far corner of Ross Island, Cape Crozier. This was the same point so wretchedly reached on foot by Cherry-Garrard, Wilson and Bowers in the winter of 1911. At first travel was laborious for Hillary and his three companions, but once the surface grew harder the team found themselves 'roaring along at six mile an hour in third gear'. At Cape Crozier they had expected to find the hut in which the earlier explorers had sheltered, but Hillary and his companion Peter Mulgrew soon found themselves sitting in their tents, drinking tea and arguing over where the hut was likely to be. To resolve their difficulty, the two men pulled out a paperback copy of *The Worst Journey in the World* and read through, line by line, Cherry-Garrard's chapter on establishing the hut. Then, still unable to agree, Hillary went one way and Mulgrew the other. Hillary climbed a spur and, in the saddle beyond, caught sight of a weathered sledge. When he clambered down, he found that the sledge was peeping over the top of an equally weathered hut, its wood polished smooth by the intervening years of wind. He was the first person to see this place since Scott's trio left it nearly 50 years before. The find had the New Zealanders 'simmering with excitement' and Hillary and his mates brought back with them a slew of abandoned items, including the sledge, three rolls of unexposed film, a blubber stove, syringes and thermometers, a tea towel and yet another tin of Cerebos salt.

In the winter they settled down to the by now venerable tradition of winter lectures. Theirs were slightly more tongue in cheek than Scott's original lecture series, however. A talk on glaciology by geologist Bernie Gunn was subtitled, 'A reasoned discourse on why ice is slippery'.

The following October Hillary and his men started on the main business of their remarkable trek. After two months, the depots that Fuchs would later use to finish his crossing were laid, and the Pole had become a tantalising prospect. So Hillary decided to keep going. His team spent Christmas Eve 1957 huddled in the caboose of their tractor train, listening to a special Radio New Zealand broadcast of messages from their wives and children. On 4 January 1958 they reached the Pole. The code word that told Scott Base of their success was suitably offbeat. It was the word 'rhubarb', that pink staple of many a New Zealand garden.

The New Zealand tractor train came to a halt outside the American base at the Pole with just 91 litres of spare fuel. Theirs were the first vehicles to drive to the South Pole, and they were the first men to reach it overland since Scott's expedition. Two months later, Fuchs arrived at Scott Base and the first full crossing of Antarctica was complete.

Hillary's expedition hut, a neatly kept retreat on the Pram Point foreshore, had failed to ignite the same awe in me as the older huts. Its utilitarian formica and wooden cupboards were too reminiscent of a recent past and it contained little in the way of exotic polar debris. Nevertheless, in an unassuming way I'm sure Hillary would approve of, the hut is being turned into a memorial to New Zealand's own heroes. During our visit, Chris had surprised me by taking a photo of a towel that still hung in the small nook where Hillary had slept. 'It's got the great man's DNA on it,' he explained.

In 2003, when researchers with the International Transantarctic Science Expedition reached the South Pole overland, the press release announcing they had made it — 45 years after Hillary — didn't even mention their names. In the future, such journeys could well become even more routine. The US has started to build a road to the Pole.

Science

The ice on the lake
Doesn't hurry or wait,
And it might be Paradise
Deep Field Song – Bill Manhire

'WE HAVE TO GET TO THE MAINLAND,' CHRIS DECLARED AS OUR group ate dinner together. There were only a couple of days left and Chris was determined that we should all step onto the continent itself, a helicopter ride away across the ice. The mountains of the mainland seemed so close in the pristine air; Chris was already frustrated at the constant clear skies. His idea of the real Antarctic experience included a blizzard. 'I don't want to be caught in one. I just want to watch it through the window,' he explained, as I tried to fathom why he would wish away the translucent blue sky.

Still, I agreed that we wouldn't know Antarctica until we had at least had a glimpse of the polar plateau, the thick compress of ice that gives Antarctica its climate of extremes. Later that evening, egged on by Chris, Tania and Vikki, I stumped across the empty dining room to where the exhausted operations manager was having a late meal. 'Jim, we want to know if we are going to the mainland,' I said. Jim looked up wearily from his meal. 'We were promised this,' I said, 'and the DVs are going.' It sounded petulant, I realised, but we were all desperate to convince him.

The next day Natalie asked us to go to the cold porch — an unheated room, as the name suggests, cluttered with machinery. There we would be weighed, she said. Though she gave no other details, we all knew that the scales were the first step to a helo flight (helicopters were never called anything other but helos here). Sure enough, two days later we were standing huddled together out by the helo pad, waiting for the American helicopter to land at Scott Base. This time our core group — Chris, Vikki, Tania, Natalie and I — was supplemented by mountaineer Jim, there to save us if we ended up stranded, and Michelle from Antarctica New Zealand. Lucrezia wasn't allowed to go as she hadn't completed the field training. I felt slightly guilty about this, since I wasn't really sure that my ineffectual attempts to stop myself in the snow, and my perfunctory shovelling, had really added much to my ability to save myself in a tight spot.

All such thoughts fled when the helo came into view and the helo technician jumped out and ran over to where we were. We huddled together for yet another briefing from the pilot's assistant. He read from a small card: we were to keep our heads low, keep the pilot in view and, if we were worried, sit down. This was a 'hot' landing, during which the rotors are kept running. We were to strap ourselves in as quickly as we could. One by one we scooted under the rotors and into the helicopter. The technician and our huts driver Spang, in his more usual role of helo support, helped bundle us in. I slipped my head into a white helmet, strapped myself in and tried not to lose my gloves out the still open door. Then Spang locked us in and retreated as the pilot boosted the engine and gently lifted us off. For a minute the helicopter hung in the air like a just-loosened dust mite, then it scuttled away across the ice shelf.

From the helicopter, we could see a straight line ruled into the ice. Scientists had been setting off explosives along that line to help them with their seismic detective work — understanding the colossal floating slab of ice beneath their feet and the earth far below it. In years to come, the scientists plan to extract sedimentary samples from that earth. Antarctica isn't just an archive of the past; it can also be a harbinger of our future. Drilling right into Antarctica's sedimentary soul just might reveal what happened last time the world warmed up. Still, this oracle can be enigmatic. Scientists have argued that the Dry Valleys — which are on the mainland, across McMurdo Sound from Ross Island, and the biggest area of ice-free land on the continent — have cooled slightly in the last 15 years or so. But temperatures on the other side of the continent have been heading in the opposite direction. On the Antarctic Peninsula, a strip of land that juts towards South

America, temperatures have risen by 0.5 degrees per decade for the past five decades. The evidence from the ice is also mixed. Scientific antennae were raised when an iceberg calved off in unusually quick time from a glacier in West Antarctica. On the other hand, the calving of supertanker icebergs from the Ross Ice Shelf — such as the one that first drew my attention to Antarctica — is thought to be a normal part of the natural ice shelf cycle. Victorian University Antarctic expert Professor Peter Barrett summed it up for me back in New Zealand: 'I think everyone agrees that parts of Antarctica are warming. There are also places that are cooling. The question is: what is happening on average.'

The concern over what could happen if climate change warms Antarctica spread beyond Antarctic specialists when the Larsen B, an ice shelf on the Antarctic Peninsula, collapsed. The Larsen B was a piece of ice about the size of Ireland, and it disintegrated into the Weddell Sea in less than a month. It was the staggering speed of the collapse that took everyone by surprise. Ice shelves, fed by the streams of ice that slough off the polar plateau, are supposed to be permanent, floating extensions of the sheets of ice that cover the continent. The Ross Ice Shelf — a much larger ice shelf about the size of France — could become vulnerable if the huge West Antarctica ice streams begin to slow or even stop. An additional threat could come from the global rise in temperatures. A United Nations panel has estimated that average global surface temperatures will rise between 1.4 and 5.8 degrees Celsius by the end of this century. All it would take, says Professor Barrett, is a rise in average global temperature of 5 degrees for the

Ross Ice Shelf to become unstable.

Even a partial collapse of the Ross Ice Shelf could be globally significant: the Ross Sea region is a source of part of the world's oceanic lifeblood — cold Antarctic bottom water. If the ice shelf were replaced by sea water, the area would absorb more heat, disturbing the flow of cold water from this region to Earth's oceans. And without the plug of the Ross Ice Shelf, the flow of the ice streams from the West Antarctic ice sheet into the Ross Sea could speed up, lifting global sea levels.

My guide to the Antarctic's sedimentary mysteries was my friend, Tim, a stellar pool player by night and a scientific star by day. 'We really understand very little about the likely future behaviour of Antarctica's large ice shelves, but we should be concerned,' he told me. With other New Zealand scientists, Tim is part of a new multinational research group called ANDRILL that aims to find out more by drilling under the Ross Ice Shelf and into the sediments beneath. It will be no easy task: at Windless Bight, part of the enormous ice plain that the explorers Scott and Shackleton had to trudge across, the New Zealand component of the ANDRILL team plans to set up the deepest drill site yet attempted in Antarctica. Getting to the sediments below will mean drilling through 200 metres of ice, then steering the drill through a kilometre of water and then digging a further kilometre into the Antarctic sediment. 'Plus [we'll be drilling] through an ice shelf that floats up and down by a metre with the tide,' observed Tim wryly.

The New Zealand scientists and their support team have managed other extraordinary feats before, however. Back in Wellington I had sat entranced through a video offering a small glimpse of the Cape Roberts drilling project — a logistical masterpiece orchestrated by Antarctic New Zealand. Each summer season for three years (1997, 1998 and 1999), a 50-tonne drilling rig and miscellaneous equipment was moved out onto the sea ice. The 40 or so people involved were fed and watered at Cape Roberts, 125 kilometres from the comforts of Scott Base. The conditions were, said one report, isolated, hostile and dangerous. Even without the overarching safety issues, there were all manner of minor indignities, including the day a seal popped out of one of the holes the team had drilled and threw up a half-eaten fish into the hut.

The isolation meant the site had to be self-sufficient. As a safety precaution, the workers were trained to dismantle the drilling rig and move it to safety on the nearby shore at Cape Roberts in less than 24 hours. One season they had to do just that. Waves were stressing the sea ice and it was breaking up — fissures were headed toward the drill site. 'This is a 50-tonne drilling rig sitting on less than two metres of ice, so you don't want to be there when that sort of thing is happening,' explained Antarctica New Zealand's Gill Wratt back in New Zealand. It took 20 hours to remove all the equipment from the ice.

The stony entrails of ancient life extracted from the drilling at Cape Roberts revealed that 17 to 34 million years ago global sea levels rose and fell by as much as 50 metres as the main — and most stable — ice sheet on the eastern side of Antarctica advanced and retreated. The climate was then three to four degrees warmer than it is today. But there are still blanks to be filled in. 'We hope to uncover the transition of the Antarctic from a warm vegetated continent without an ice sheet, about 35 million years ago, into a colder continent with the first ice sheets developing,' Tim explained to me.

The season I was there, the ANDRILL project was just beginning. The first step was seismic exploration: hard, hard work planting explosives, digging in instruments and hauling cables over 38 kilometres of ice. Along the cable, the team had to line up geophones, instruments that eavesdropped on the aftermath of small explosions in the ice shelf. The seismic waves from the explosions travelled down through the snow, through the 200-metre-thick ice shelf and then down even further, through a thousand metres of water to bounce back off the sea floor. The geophones picked up the tiny differences between the return of each wave and shot the data back along the cable to the waiting scientists. Measuring those tiny differences in the seismic waves would allow the scientists to construct a picture of the sea floor below the thick slab of ice.

I had met Stephen, the geophysicist who was deciphering the seismic data, back at the base, where he spent long hours bent over his laptop. Stephen livened up one long evening with his description of a science camp on the ice. He confided that he had been a bit of a tyrant out there, pushing everyone to work hard, which often meant that they lost weight. 'They called it Stephen's Antarctic health camp,' he told me, smiling genially.

It was the scientists who surprised me the most in Antarctica. Somehow I had got it into my head that they would be fusty, bearded men, ordering assistants to carry out obscure tasks. Instead I met bright, charming and, in the main, young women and men, out in the field trying to push the boundaries of science. That they were here at all was the result of the Antarctic Treaty, which in its first article reserves the continent for peace and, in its second, upholds the freedom of scientific investigation. Part of the push for New Zealand's first official sally south in the late 1950s had come from the scientific community; they wanted to ensure that New Zealand scientists took part in a year of global scientific effort called the International Geophysical Year. The IGY was to concentrate on Earth's poles. Scientists were to travel to the ice alongside much-lauded explorers in the interests of ground-breaking research. The leader of that first group of scientists was Dr Trevor Hatherton, after whom the Scott Base laboratory is named. According to Antarctic historian Leslie Quartermain, Hatherton and the four others in that original science team did their full share of chores alongside the support staff at the base — 'naturally, being New Zealanders'.

Forty-odd years on, collegial intermingling continues, but scientists are now having to adapt to more and more intrusions into their world. Travelling between Scott Base and McMurdo we had overheard a conversation between Jim, the operations manager, and one of the scientists we were scheduled to visit. Apparently, the next day was crucial for his team's experiments and the scientist wanted to change the time of our visit. The thrust of those delicate negotiations — anyone could listen in to the radio telephone link — was that having to entertain visitors cut into the scientists' limited time on the ice. The counter-argument was that such visits allowed those favoured to take away a fresh appreciation of the work the scientists were doing. Eventually, the scientist agreed to our visit. I was worried about our reception, but when we arrived the science team was only too happy to share their work and their time.

On our way out to see the huts of Scott and Shackleton, we had visited the site of a team studying the algae found on the underside of the sea ice. The expansion and melting of the sea ice around Antarctica is the single biggest surface change, in terms of mass and energy, on Earth each year. Ken Ryan, the team's leader, explained it to us: 'If you can imagine, there's maybe 20 million square kilometres of sea ice that covers the sea all around Antarctica. By the end of the season, by February or March, maybe four million square kilometres are left. That's a huge amount of ice and all of it's got this sort of algae growing in it. It all melts and drops down into the water and becomes part of the food chain.' This particular season Ken and his team were looking at how UVB radiation affected sea ice algae. To my untrained eye, the method looked quite simple: differing plastics were laid over the sea ice; in some areas fluorescent tubes boosted the amount of radiation the sea ice was exposed to. The scientists had found that the UVB did seem to have an impact on the sea ice algae, but the significance of this research, like so much else in Antarctica, would reach far beyond algae. The scientists plan to extend the techniques they have developed to look at what impact higher temperatures would have on the myriad other creatures that rely for life on the water under that ice.

We wandered around the sea ice and looked into their office — actually one of the shipping containers that provide the shelter for the scientific team. Inside they showed us videos of their work. Floating across the screens was a fiesta of tiny, unimaginably delicate algae. This was the inspiration for artist Virginia King's twirling sculptures of diatoms.

The scientists' passion for the work they were doing in this austere, remote place was clear — and catching. 'Sometimes we've seen little shrimps just grazing on this stuff like sheep,' said Ken of his algae. He showed us a video of a block of ice, about two metres thick, being cut from the ice. 'It's a big lump of ice. It's really quite beautiful.' Enraptured, I murmured 'amen' to that.

Outside on the ice, we were invited to help extract a core of ice. The first step is to drill a hole into the ice — not easy when the drill was taller than me. Inside the puncture made by the drill goes the corer, a larger version of an apple corer. We took turns winding the coring device into the sea ice until the water thrust its way up through the hole. On the bottom of the cylinder of ice they extracted was the algae the scientists were studying. Arms aching from our exertions, we all snapped photos of our very first ice core.

Creature comforts help ease the isolation of these scientific outposts: one camp we visited had a bread maker. The height of luxury, however, was the science camp that had a proper toilet, complete with its own small room. Natalie and Spang had called into this camp on our day trip to the historic huts to avoid having to subject us again to the waning delights of the pee pole. The camp consisted of a neat row of shipping containers housing the accommodation, kitchen and laboratories. In the accommodation area, brightly coloured curtains, knocked up at home in New Zealand out of material designed for children, separated off each bunk. Here was someone with a sense of mischief, and that impression was reinforced when I found out that this camp had produced one of the first nude Antarctic calendars. The scientists had posed on the great slabs of ice they dug up and studied. Sadly, the camp was rather deserted when we were there — some people were away working elsewhere; some were back at Scott Base. One of the younger scientists did take the time to show us his work on sea ice. Under his microscope was a crystalline sliver of one of those huge blocks of ice — revealed by polarising filters as a dazzling kaleidoscope of colour. I stood there wondering if I could make crazy patterns by twisting the eyepiece.

Outside, Tania and Vikki had jollied our young scientist into allowing them to drive the two-seater vehicle parked nearby. It was an Argo, an amphibious all-terrain vehicle, and Tania and Vikki took turns madly spinning the Argo around in ever tighter circles on the ice.

A short drive away from Scott Base at Arrival Heights, in a building cluttered with monitoring equipment, New Zealand's National Institute of Water and Atmospheric Research keeps tabs on the ozone hole that has begun to appear each summer over Antarctica. During my teenage years, my notion of sun care revolved round lathering on the coconut oil to promote that essential summer fashion accessory, a tan. These days, our morning routine includes smothering the children in sunscreen and every month or so I diligently check my many freckles and moles for cancerous inclinations. At the Arrival Heights laboratory, a huge white machine helps to measure the ozone in the air above. It is measured in Dobson units, explained Dan, the technician who monitored the machines. The Dobson machine, a spectrograph, was the invention of British meteorologist Gordon Dobson. The first one was made in 1924, and the one at Arrival Heights is number 17. Dobson Number 17 clearly has a place in Dan's heart. 'It's all cast iron. It's real craftsmanship,' he told us. The measurements were scratched out on wax paper. On a low ozone day, Dan warns field parties visiting the laboratory to slap on some extra sun block.

The US laboratory at nearby McMurdo Station is, of course, huge by comparison. The local legend is that the Crary Lab — 4320 square metres, three floors and 19 laboratories — is the most expensive in the world per square metre. It was also one of the most comfortable buildings — in terms of static electricity — on Ross Island. To avoid damaging expensive equipment with static discharges, the laboratory has been humidified to 30 percent. Each season about 80 scientists use the base, we were told as we toured the lab. It seemed hard to believe, as we moved from one equipment-filled room to the next, that sometimes US scientists either took their work home or brought equipment along because Crary didn't have what they needed. So, being just around the hill from McMurdo has another advantage for New Zealand scientists; many team up with their US counterparts on research projects, gaining entry to the Crary Lab.

Our tour of Crary — the weekly public tour — took us down through the wide white lab corridors to the marine section. There I dipped my hand warily into the freezing waters of a touch pool full of Antarctic marine life. A plump orange starfish was splayed on the bottom of the tank and small fish with frilly fins darted from side to side. A larger tank held a huge Antarctic cod swimming monotonously around and around, its eyes glassy and huge slit of a mouth menacing. These fish survive in the freezing temperatures of the waters around Antarctica because a protein in their blood acts as an antifreeze agent. The American scientist who discovered those antifreeze properties was a 40-year institution here, returning every year to unravel more mysteries of Antarctic marine life. The fish in the tank have a more prosaic use as well: once they've been studied, our tour guide told us, they end up on the McMurdo dinner menu as sushi.

As our helo shuttled us briskly across the ice, the two American pilots tried good-naturedly to engage us in conversation over our headsets. For me, though, adding conversation to my concentrated contemplation of the marvels around me was just too much. Down towards the south we could see Black and White Islands, marooned in the ice. Far off in the distance was Minna Bluff: when that landmark disappeared from view to the south, bad weather was coming. To the north were icebergs, chunks of texture trapped in the larger expanse of sea ice.

Our destination that day was the Dry Valleys, elongated brown deserts that run from McMurdo Sound towards the polar plateau, forming little nicks in the Transantarctic Mountains. A team led by Robert Scott first saw this weird landscape in the Taylor Valley back in 1903. Members of

Shackleton's 1907–09 expedition explored the Ferrar and Upper Taylor glaciers in 1909, but it wasn't until the 1950s that serious exploration got under way. The valleys were mapped from the air, then a group of five New Zealanders, including two third-year geology students who had wangled their way onto the expedition, made the first extensive geological and biological survey. It was the beginning of a long quest to unravel the mysteries of the valleys.

Before we reached them, however, we were to make a visit to New Harbour to see another New Zealand science team. This time, they were studying life on the sea floor of coastal Antarctica. The only way to observe these benthic communities was to dive into waters that were almost two degrees below freezing. When we arrived we were ushered into an American diving hut in the shape of a semi-circular tube, similar to the Coffee House back at McMurdo. The Americans, who had returned to McMurdo, were letting the New Zealand team use their huts. Like their other accommodation here, the American diving hut was a step up from the small New Zealand tents next door. Above the main hut, in a salute to the expedition flags of the past, the brightly coloured flags of the US expedition were displayed.

Inside the hut, two scientists dressed in bright red wetsuits, yellow cylinders strapped to their backs, sat with their legs dangling into a hole cut in the ice, getting ready for their next immersion. For some reason I still clung to the belief that the scientists would get someone else to do the difficult work, but I was beginning to understand that part of the attraction of being a scientist in Antarctic *was* the difficult stuff. The athletic-looking, 30-something woman and man togging up to dive were not only expert divers — these frigid waters allowed no room for error — they were also brimful of academic prowess. A third diver, also togged out in all the gear, was supervising from the top of the hole, ready to plunge in should the divers need help fast. As a further safety measure, the divers were attached to a rope. The rope could extend up to 50 metres from the hole, but even so it was, the divers said, a long way back to the hole if something happened. As with everything else in Antarctica, the unexpected was built into the system: a second hole was cut into the ice under the hut, just in case a seal decided to occupy the divers' hole.

In the Antarctic water, manifold layers of clothing are worn, just as they are outside it. 'We have really thick polyprop underwear. Then we have a kind of bunny suit, a one-piece fleece, and then we have a dry suit with a wetsuit over that. What insulates us is of course the air trapped [in the layers]. And then we have big double twin tanks and fins and goggles,' explained one of the scientists.

The two divers slipped through the film of ice constantly re-forming over the hole. One diver videoed his companion as she measured the algae on the underside of the sea ice. When it covers the ice thickly enough, the algae gives the ice an unearthly green sheen. In the huts I stood transfixed by a small video monitor showing the divers weaving their way through the flora and fauna of the sea floor community. They stayed in the water up to 45 minutes; any longer and the divers start to succumb to the cold and become befuddled. Keeping within the time limit means only the tips of their fingers and their lips start to go numb. Headaches, like the ones you get after eating ice cream, are another hazard. It was hard, one of the divers told us, to get past the logistics and the gear of this research to get to the science. But, for all the sophistication of the divers' preparations, some things were kept simple. To trap warmth inside the divers' gloves, a piece of string was tucked between the wrist seal and the glove to let in a trickle of air.

This was the science team's second camp that summer. They had been over at Cape Evans earlier, doing much the same work, which will also feed into another major New Zealand-led project, the Latitudinal Gradient Project. The idea of this project is to look at changes to Antarctic environments along the coast from south to north. The differing micro-climates are intended to give the scientists a proxy for climate change.

We were ready to leave the New Harbour camp, but it turned out that a door on the helo wouldn't shut. The pilot and his assistant could probably have fixed the problem themselves, but that was against the rules, so a mechanic was flown over in another helo from McMurdo. We waited in the camp's kitchen hut, where I eyed up the Americans' vast supply of chocolate. I was dissuaded from helping myself, though. Apparently the American science team's generous sharing of their campsite didn't extend to food supplies. The helicopter fixed, we loaded up and headed for the firm earth of the Dry Valleys.

We would fly up the Taylor Valley first and then down the Wright Valley. Here the ice was sporadic — the mountains have managed to dam up most of the ice sheet. These brown oases are so desolate, they are the closest thing on Earth to the landscape of Mars.

On either side of the valley were brown-grey hills. In some places the mountains seemed to slide gently down to the valley floor; in others, the crags would have made a vertiginous climb. My geology lectures echoed in my head as I peered out at mountaintops where the history of Antarctica could be read in precise brown layers. The light tan was a type of sandstone and the black was ferrar dolerite, volcanic magma that had elbowed its way through the Beacon sandstone about 160 million years ago.

Also clamouring for our stunned attention were rivers of ice, jostling through any opening the mountains would give them. On either side of the valley as we approached, we saw first one, then another, then another, huge glacier. Some eased themselves over the ridgeline, antimacassars for the mountains, but two giants oozed down onto the valley floor, as if just freshly squeezed from a tube of malleable ice. In New Zealand any one of these glaciers would have been an exclamation mark on the landscape; here they were fat white commas punctuating our flight.

The head of the valley quickly reared up, and there, finally, was the polar plateau. Rapacious winds were hurling snow over the ice sheet, repelling any advance towards what was literally the end of the Earth. In the distance, the blue sky and ice seemed to merge into one, blurring into an endless horizon. Spreading along the edge of the plateau was a waterfall of ice that seemed to be hesitating briefly in its inexorable trek towards the coast from the South Pole. Rivulets surged over the edge to join the lagoon of ice below. It was through this desolate, awful beauty those first explorers had trudged, their faces turned into the endless southerly.

Then, suddenly, the plateau was gone, as the pilot swung the helicopter over the mountains and dropped down into the neighbouring valley. Nestled into the hollows of the valley floor were little frozen pools, and then one that wasn't frozen and, even more out of place, that had a reflection. This was the Don Juan Pond, a reservoir for water that is reputedly the saltiest in the world. It is so saline, in fact, that it never freezes, even when the temperature falls to 50 degrees below Celsius. The pond, discovered just 40 years earlier, was named for two pilots who were members of the first field party to study the pond: one named Donald and the other John. They decided that using plain John wouldn't be quite right, our pilot told us, so it became Don Juan. I wished that a similar sensitivity had been applied to the magnificent icefalls we had seen earlier. They were named after the US Navy squadron that has supported so much Antarctic exploration, the US Navy Air Development Squadron Six. And so these beautiful pendants of ice now went by the sturdily unromantic name Airdevronsix Icefalls.

We flew over a labyrinthine section of dolerite, its twists and turns apparently scoured by water. It was not the only fantastic shape: below we could also see polygonal shapes highlighted by a dusting of snow on parts of the valley floor. The patterns on the ground were a by-product of the permafrost below the surface of the soil. Mars couldn't be any weirder, I decided.

Our next destination, and our only stop on the continent, was Lake Vanda, nestled between the sweeping walls of the Wright Valley. For nearly 30 years, from 1969 to 1995, it was home to a New Zealand station and a few green sheds are still kept there for scientific use. The New Zealand camp was removed after the rising lake waters began to encroach on the buildings. It was feared that they, and the soil surrounding them, might contaminate the lake. Such concern for the environment hasn't always been in evidence. Gaining membership of the Vanda Swim Club after a naked dip in the lake was a badge of belonging for many who visited the New Zealand camp. Back in Wellington I had seen a picture of a helicopter dipping its floats into the lake's little sullied waters. In 1987, the environmental lobby group Greenpeace set up a base near Scott's Cape Evans hut. Their aim was to have Antarctica deemed a world park. That aim wasn't achieved, but the treaty nations did agree to the Protocol on Environmental Protection in 1991. The next year Greenpeace dismantled its Antarctic base.

In the same year I visited the ice, Antarctica New Zealand produced a 280-page report on the state of the environment in the Ross Sea region, the first report of its type for any part of Antarctica. For the most part, the region was still pristine, the report declared: 'exceptionally so by global standards'. But it also pointed out that the short history of modern Antarctic research leaves significant gaps in knowledge about most aspects of the area.

Climate change and ozone depletion, the focus of many of the sophisticated scientific enquiries we had seen, were judged to be the major threats to the Ross Sea ecosystems. The biggest question marks for the region are the fledgling tourism industry and fishing. In the part of the Southern Ocean overseen by New Zealand, fishing crews are already enduring the harsh conditions of the two-month fishing season for the promise of Patagonian toothfish, a catch so lucrative that it has been called 'white gold'. Independent tourists are still few in number, but the restoration of the Heroic Age huts could well prove to be an irresistible lure for well-heeled travellers. Even the relatively small number of people who visit the Ross Sea region now have an impact, despite the rapidly increasing environmental awareness. In the Dry Valleys, we had been warned to take care where we walked. A careless step could snuff out lichens that had been clinging tenaciously to the valley floor for more than a thousand years.

The helo wafted gently down to the ground, the rotors shut down and we clambered out. The gravel beneath my feet was a welcome respite after so much ice. We walked first to see a mummified seal, its long sleek body desiccated by the dry atmosphere. It looked like a piece of driftwood marooned in a strange sea. Natalie said no one was quite sure how it ended up so far from the ocean. It may have just become confused and wandered up here thousands of years ago. Or it could have been dragged here by pranksters. An empty eye socket glared up at me as I bent down to photograph its face.

Suddenly there was no time to linger. Our minder Natalie urged us over to the lake for the ultimate Antarctic tourism photo. We walked carefully. I was looking out for lichens and briefly thought about picking up just one of the sleek black stones lying so temptingly at my feet as a memento. The stern warning in my itinerary — no natural materials will be taken — reverberated in my head. No natural materials could be left, either, so I was glad I did not need to go to the toilet here. It wouldn't have meant the intricacies of a pee pole, but rather the indignity of a pee bottle.

The lake, the palest pastel blue we had yet seen, was cradled in the broad brown sweep of the mountains that framed the valley. Its surface was a cracked film of ice — like huge ice cubes squashed together. Cautiously, I stepped out onto the crust of the lake. It looked as if I could easily fall through the maze of fractured patterns, but the ice beneath me was firm. I skidded carefully towards the others, who were peering intently downwards. Dotted throughout the ice were tiny globules of what looked like snow. They were, explained Natalie, trapped bubbles of air. Below the mantle of ice, brown algae could be seen. The algae were about two metres down, but they looked just centimetres away. I was so entranced by the shattered ice beneath my feet that I only remembered to ask Chris to snap just one photo of me on the ice. I stood still, shouted 'Yikla!', and then, the photograph taken, we had to go.

On the way back to Ross Island we stopped to refuel the helicopter on the edge of the ice shelf. From out of a ramshackle collection of buildings, an American attendant emerged to help the pilot fill up.

Return

Before a face or a landscape
Has power to shape or destroy
I'm Older than You, Please Listen – A R D Fairburn

MY LAST ANTARCTIC DAY STARTED EARLY: MY HEAD WAS WHIRLING with thoughts of leaving my crystal cocoon, and from the effects of the night before. The weather had felt so warm when we returned the previous evening — just 10 degrees below zero — that we sat out on the deck for a while, soaking up the view. I even toyed with the idea of eating my dinner outside. After dinner, Tania, Vikki and I decided on one last Antarctica first. We decided to try the Scott Base hot tub. In a shed outside, some ingenious engineer had turned the inside of an old snow-melting machine into a steamy bath. There was a small changing room and a mural of the tropics on one wall. We were already sitting quietly soaking, the hot tub soothing away the various pains in my muscles, when we noticed that a briefing was required before use. We decided to ignore our transgression and hoped that Natalie would, too.

Holes along one of the pipes in the tub had been rigged to turn the hot pool into a spa, of sorts. A biggish hole in one of the pipes meant that the effect was more volcanic than soothing, but we soon had a *modus operandi* worked out. One of us had to deposit our bottom over the big hole while another pressed the button. 'Ready, mate?' asked Tania. 'Ready, Tarn,' I replied, perched firmly over the hole. The bubbles erupted, flinging me off the pipe, and we subsided into helpless laughter.

As a final flourish, we decided to amplify the heat of the hot tub with a quick dash outside into the snow. We took care to leave the door open; our wet skin would have stuck to the metal door handles. Then we wrapped up in towels to dash past the bar.

That night we bought drinks for everyone in the bar. It was a Sunday night, so there weren't many people there late. And perhaps we hadn't followed the correct procedure for a 'shout'. Wearing a hat, boots, or any other item of ECW gear, as well as ringing the bell at the door, usually precedes a call for a shout. But we ordered up a few bottles of champagne anyway and tried to persuade the base manager to keep the bar open, without success. Despite our efforts to rustle up a party, everyone sensibly started to drift off to bed.

Undeterred, we rifled through the eclectic album collection.

I was convinced that some of them must have been among the 500 vinyl records sent down with Sir Edmund Hillary's Transantarctic Expedition party in 1957. They were given one record for every day they were supposed to be in Antarctica. I think most of them are still there — it seems nothing ever goes back to New Zealand. A scratchy selection of Maori love songs gave way to a battered version of *Hotel California*, the seminal Eagles album (seminal for 40-somethings anyway). A few days later, back home, I realised just how apt that song was for Antarctic visitors. Others who had been before me had warned that you never quite leave.

We had begun to hope that our departure would be delayed by bad weather. The temperature was rising — a sign that bad weather might be about to arrive. Natalie kept us on our scheduled track, however: we packed our bags and hauled them down to the cold porch.

Our flight wasn't leaving till later that afternoon, so we spent the morning at McMurdo, talking to the helo manager, the doctor and the weather service manager. Since 1996, a civilian company had provided the US helicopters in the Antarctic. New Zealand sent down one helo each summer season; it was coming in the plane that was taking us home. Flying in Antarctica, the helo manager told us, was the best flying in the world, even though strange tricks of the light could flummox pilots. Apparently, flying in all that white could be 'like flying inside a ping-pong ball'. But his was a conservative profession: he always liked to bring home the same number of people he left with. The versatility of helos meant they were in high demand in Antarctica. 'Geologists always want to see the rock over the next hill,' he explained. But flying time is expensive and rationed — we realised just how lucky we had been to have had our flight to the Dry Valleys.

For the McMurdo doctor, the work was mainly routine, but, with a couple of thousand people on site, he expected a heart attack at least once a season. The heavy machinery around the station also means that there was the potential for people to get 'critically crunched'. McMurdo has an emergency room, but anyone with serious injuries gets airlifted back to Christchurch. The station doctor had had plenty of opportunity to admire the skills and adaptability of his Antarctic colleagues. His X-ray machine was fixed at the South Pole by an engineering graduate from the prestigious Massachusetts Institute of Technology, working in Antarctica in some much more lowly role. Whatever it took to get to the ice, it seemed. As we rode one of the bloated American buses back to Scott Base later that day, we joked none too quietly that our driver was probably a brain surgeon back home. Finally, unburdening himself to strangers, the doctor began to rail against the rules at McMurdo — far stricter it seemed than those at Scott Base: 'You sign out in duplicate just to go pee on yellow flags.' The constant, but relatively relaxed, safety briefings at Scott Base didn't seem quite so bad after all.

Our last stop at McMurdo was the weather operations centre. Every morning, the day's weather, as analysed by McMurdo, was pinned up on the Scott Base mess noticeboard. It was essential reading, since the weather dictated the timing of everything else in the Antarctic. 'Normal' weather was rated condition three; only the usual travel precautions were required for condition three weather. Normal here meant that severe weather was possible within 24 to 48 hours. If the weather was condition two (Caution), then the wind could blow up to 100 kilometres an hour, visibility was going to be less than 300 metres and the wind chill could take the temperature down to minus 73 degrees Celsius. In condition two weather people moving about on foot were restricted to areas around the base; anyone wanting to travel by vehicle in condition two had to get a manager's approval. Condition one weather was rated Danger, and everyone stayed in. In Antarctica, winds of more than 100 kilometres an hour and wind-chill temperatures lower than 73 degrees Celsius constituted 'danger'.

The US meteorologists we met had the job of distilling that information for everyone living below 60 degrees South. Their information came from seven satellites on a polar orbit and automated weather stations dotted around the continent. This information, said the met service manager, was made available for free. They had to pay for the information they needed from their New Zealand counterparts, he said rather pointedly. I scanned the swirling images on the screen, hoping to see evidence of the bad weather the meteorologists were expecting. The rising temperature and the lack of wind were signals of an impending change. As a precaution, our Starlifter was being held in Christchurch until they were more confident of the outlook. We all wanted Chris's blizzard to arrive now.

We needed to find transport back to Scott Base, but I baulked at having to make the radio call ordering a ute. I hadn't come here to learn to use a radio, I snarled. I was getting tetchy. Tania came to the rescue and made the call, but there were no utes or drivers available and we were told to catch the next American shuttle bus. I slouched on the bench of the bus shelter. It had a sign above it saying Derelict Junction. Disconsolate Junction was more like it.

Back at Scott Base we eked out the rest of the day. I shopped at the store, buying flannels and T-shirts adorned with penguins for the kids; two fleecy jackets labelled Scott Base for Simon and me; and calendars and mugs for everyone else. I also bought a couple of bottles of Scott Base wine. The merchandise, of course, had all been flown into Scott Base. The wine, though never left New Zealand. I was instructed to pick up my bottle when I dropped my clothing back at the depot in Christchurch.

I tracked down Mike, the station manager, and obtained that coveted passport stamp: a little square containing the face of a penguin and Mike's official-looking date stamp. I also posted nine envelopes given to me by a philatelic friend of the family. The 50 cent Ross Dependency stamp depicted Scott's Hut at Cape Evans. Nowadays all the letters from Antarctica are flown to Christchurch where they are postmarked by the Ross Dependency agency; gone is the exclusive cachet of the Scott Base Post Office. The stamp enthusiast had carefully labelled the letter, 'Visit of Kim Griggs, Journalist, to Antarctic Bases.' I had signed below that, as he had requested. Later one of these neatly prepared envelopes was returned to me. I was to keep it safe, my Mum's stamp-collecting friend told me. It was, after all, one of only nine in the world.

By now there was one thing left to do that I felt I had the energy for. So, instead of making the climb up scree-covered

Observation Hill to remember Scott, I climbed the stairs to the Scott Base library. Locked in a glass cabinet were the private, personal memories of the families of the 257 people who had died on the mountain just beyond the library window. Few of the families of those killed on Erebus have been able to see where their loved ones are buried; two decades after the tragedy, this book provided some closure for them. One of the lecturers on my Antarctic course had been the public relations officer at Scott Base in the summer of 1979, a job that as a budding journalist I had once coveted. He had captured an Air New Zealand DC-10 on film, high above Scott Base on 7 November 1979. Three weeks later, on 28 November, 1979, he again waited for the flight, hoping for a shot of the koru, the unfurling fern that is the Air New Zealand logo, against the clear Antarctic sky. He thought the advertising people at Air New Zealand would snap it up. Instead, his enduring photographic legacy is a grainy black and white image of the torn koru-emblazoned tail of Air New Zealand TE901 lying amid the crash-site debris.

I had been annoyed at my father when he called that day in America to tell me that the plane was missing. He had woken the family I was staying with in California because he had the time zones wrong. I was, at nineteen, embarrassed by my family's lack of travel sophistication. Once home, I introduced my cousins to olives and chastised my father. It was my last argument with him; he died suddenly just eight weeks later. As melancholy threatened to overwhelm me, I noted that the explanatory note next to the cabinet had the date of the crash wrong.

Waiting to find out if our delayed plane was going to be

able to come in, it was hard to settle to anything. Tania, Vikki and I decided to go for one last walk on the sea ice outside the base. We signed out, but failed to take a radio, flouting the rules Natalie had worked so hard to ingrain in us. At least we followed the flags as we set off to walk around the sculpted ridges of ice that swelled up just off Pram Point. These were pressure ridges, uplifted as the ice shelf pushed against Ross Island. Their strange curves had the look of surf curling in towards the beach.

Determined to gain some mastery over the ice, I took off my coat and tried a forward roll on the ice. Not satisfied with that small success, I decided to attempt a headstand. I deposited my hat on the ice, positioned my arms, and put my head down on top of the hat. After watching with growing incredulity as I failed to lift my feet anywhere near the vertical, Tania grabbed my mukluks and hauled my legs up. Vikki, giggling, took photos of each stage of my awkward gymnastics. Time was ticking away, so we turned to walk back to the base. But mere walking didn't seem sufficient to burn, for one final time, the ice images into my memory. I lay down and stared at the wide, wide sky. The air smelt of nothing at all. Back at the base, Chris was still bemoaning the lack of blizzard, but I was resigned to leaving. I silently gave thanks to Roald's nose, back at the Canterbury museum, glad that the weather had stayed perfect.

Eventually, we heard that our plane had left New Zealand to head south. Once it was past its point of no return, we knew we would be departing that day. We had our final dinner in the mess and I made a few awkward farewells before joining the others in the utes to be transported once again out to the ice runway.

There was a rudimentary waiting room there, but for a while we all hung around outside, waiting to see the Starlifter arrive. It was cloudy; the mountains were a smudged line between the cloud and the ice. At last a tiny black silhouette that was the Starlifter came into view against the mountainous backdrop, descended slowly, landed and then taxied to a halt down the other end of the runway from us. I felt forlorn as I watched the new arrivals being bundled into the New Zealand utes. We waved as they left; I doubt anyone noticed us.

Tania, Vikki, Chris and I cajoled someone to take one last photo of us with the herd of Hercules in the background. Inside the waiting room an American woman was directing the loading of the passengers and scooped up Lucrezia in one of the first groups. This time around there were no boarding passes — there was only one flight north — but the loading of passengers was delayed while they struggled to remove the New Zealand helicopter from the back of the plane. We ended up waiting for four hours in the airport buildings before they finally managed to extract it. I wondered whether Lucrezia had ended up on the right plane and Tania joked that she was probably heading to the South Pole right now.

When we finally got aboard, however, Lucrezia was there before us. This time round the webbing was slung down both sides of the plane and the empty hold meant we had endless space. We were travelling with the same crew that had brought us down, but none of us bothered with the flight deck and only managed limited conversation. The heaters were turned

149

up full blast, so once the plane had taken off I stretched out and went to sleep.

It was 4 a.m. by the time we arrived in New Zealand. The stars of the Southern Cross were slung low in the sky. The air was soft, warm and moist. We were loaded into buses to cross the tarmac and I grabbed one of the front seats, next to one of the latest batch of DVs. I wondered vaguely if I was bucking some seating arrangement, but by this time I no longer cared.

Inside the terminal, waiting for our bags, we shed our layers of protective clothing and emerged from our blue Antarctic skins. Putting on a seatbelt without a safety briefing in the car outside the terminal felt vaguely wicked, and that gave Tania, Vikki and I a last laugh, tinged with sadness. I was dropped off and bade farewell to my friends. It had been so hot in the plane that I showered before falling into my first decent sleep for a week.

In the damp of the New Zealand morning, my hair curled.

Back home again I struggled to adjust to the pallid sky and green hills outside the living room window. I began the slow task of trying to fit my life back into the family calendar stuck to my refrigerator. I walked my daughters to school; I waved to the other mothers who beeped a welcome as they drove past. I scanned the live picture of Scott Base on the Internet most days, and Tania, Vikki, Chris and I kept up a constant flow of email. I wasn't ready to stop being the person I had conjured up in the isolation of Antarctica.

I bought a set of juggling balls as a small gift for the people at the base. I enjoyed the symbolism of it — they had, I felt, juggled me expertly for a week, never once letting me fall. I rang Woody to check if they would be okay to send: the balls were covered with brightly coloured leather, so as not to be lost in the snow. It was only later that I worried about the stuffing: polystyrene filling or seeds are a big no-no in Antarctica.

Now I needed to begin the search for words that could frame my experience, so I turned to one of my favourite New Zealand poets, the curmudgeonly A.R.D. Fairburn. I had kept his poetry with me while I was living and travelling overseas: his poem for the war dead had comforted me when a friend died far too young from the ravages of Aids; his mournful poem for expatriates was pulled out whenever wine and homesickness overcame me. But it was his entreaty — which I had once taken so seriously — to the young of New Zealand to leave the country 'before a face or a landscape had power to shape or destroy' that I chanced on now. In Antarctica, Fairburn's exhortation had no validity. The continent's powerful landscape did not seep gently into the soul; it transfixed you, seized you, the moment you arrived. This was no gentle romance, it was a geographical *coup de foudre*. Here, there was simply no before.

Though the impressive resources of modern technology have been brought to bear on a tiny corner of Antarctica, it remains an untamed icy wilderness, its vast emptiness allowing everyone who goes there a fresh palette. And for New Zealand it is a place where we can be drawn large. Despite our relatively small presence in our slice of Antarctica, New Zealand scientists are leading major projects. Antarctica New Zealand is active in the ongoing political life of Antarctica and the Antarctic circle has widened in recent years to enable New Zealand artists and writers to interpret the continent on canvas and page. The Antarctic has had some impact on almost everyone in New Zealand. It is, after all, our only southern neighbour. During one of my lectures, poet Bill Manhire had likened Antarctica to Australia's Outback: it hovered at the edge of everyone's psyche, even if it was never visited.

The month after I returned I decided that Simon and the girls had to know more about what I had experienced, so we all caught the ferry to Picton and drove to Christchurch for a weekend to see the tourist version of Antarctica at the International Antarctic Centre. The first room we entered was a dazzling display of sound and light, recreating the fury of the Antarctic blizzard I never experienced. The main hall featured an array of Antarctic machinery, displays and videos. Most thrilling for the girls was the chill room, packed with machine-made ice to give the feel of the Antarctic without leaving Christchurch. Before entering we bundled up in extreme-cold-weather coats and special shoes. Inside, the girls climbed on a stationary skidoo, huddled in a snow cave, slid down a small hill of ice and braved the wind machines to find out what wind chill felt like. Simon took photos and the girls told anyone that would listen that their Mum had been to Antarctica. They weren't then sick of hearing about the 'cold place'.

Earlier that day I had been to the suburban Christchurch home of an Antarctic devotee. For years David has stuffed his suburban shed with modern memorabilia from Antarctica.

His fridge houses a 19-year-old block of ice from Lake Vanda. Visitors sit in an old Scott Base office chair and all manner of flags, boots, hats and posters insulate the walls against the Christchurch cold. If the phone rings in the Polar Room, as the shed is grandly named, David likes to try to trick newcomers into believing that the call has come direct from Scott Base.

Before we left, David pressed his visitors' book into my hands. It seemed my entry would precede that of Sir Edmund Hillary, who was scheduled to visit later that same afternoon. Though I felt my insignificance next to the great man, I signed 'Yikla' with a flourish. Posed in the Scott Base chair for the mandatory photo, I felt anointed as an Antarctican.

Further Reading

For the ultimate Heroic Age saga, look no further than Aspley
Cherry-Garrard's *The Worst Journey in the World* (Picador).
All the grim grandeur of Antarctica is here.

To revel in the japes and camaraderie that marked those
first Heroic Age voyages, I suggest *The Voyages of the Morning*
(Bluntisham Books/Erskine Press), by Gerald Doorly.

Readers seeking modern-day Antarctica should lap up Sara
Wheeler's *Terra Incognita* (Vintage). Intending travellers can
explore the continent via Lonely Planet's *Antarctica*.

Two authors have kept New Zealand's history in Antarctica
to the fore. L.B. Quartermain's *New Zealand and the Antarctic*
(New Zealand Government Printer) is a classic. David
Harrowfield keeps the modern Kiwi flame alive in *The Tip of
the Iceberg: Yarns and Ditties of New Zealanders in Antarctica*
(South Latitude Research).

All manner of Antarctic facts can be found in *Antarctica:*

An Encyclopaedia from Abbott Ice Shelf to Zooplankton (David Bateman). Another excellent omnibus of Antarctic detail is *The Complete Story: Antarctica* (Random House New Zealand). Anyone keen on words should enjoy perusing *The Antarctica Dictionary* (CSIRO Publishing), by Bernadette Hince.

For a more surreal take on Antarctica, try Kim Stanley Robinson's *Antarctica* (Voyager), or Edgar Allan Poe's *The Narrative of Arthur Gordon Pym of Nantucket* (Penguin). Delight in poetic perfection by reading Bill Manhire's 'Antarctic Field Notes' in his *Collected Poems* (Victoria University Press).